POACHING AND TERRORISM: A NATIONAL SECURITY CHALLENGE

HEARING

BEFORE THE

SUBCOMMITTEE ON TERRORISM, NONPROLIFERATION, AND TRADE

OF THE

COMMITTEE ON FOREIGN AFFAIRS HOUSE OF REPRESENTATIVES

ONE HUNDRED FOURTEENTH CONGRESS

FIRST SESSION

APRIL 22, 2015

Serial No. 114–25

Printed for the use of the Committee on Foreign Affairs

Available via the World Wide Web: http://www.foreignaffairs.house.gov/ or http://www.gpo.gov/fdsys/

U.S. GOVERNMENT PUBLISHING OFFICE

94–308PDF   WASHINGTON : 2015

For sale by the Superintendent of Documents, U.S. Government Publishing Office
Internet: bookstore.gpo.gov   Phone: toll free (866) 512–1800; DC area (202) 512–1800
Fax: (202) 512–2104   Mail: Stop IDCC, Washington, DC 20402–0001

COMMITTEE ON FOREIGN AFFAIRS

EDWARD R. ROYCE, California, *Chairman*

CHRISTOPHER H. SMITH, New Jersey	ELIOT L. ENGEL, New York
ILEANA ROS-LEHTINEN, Florida	BRAD SHERMAN, California
DANA ROHRABACHER, California	GREGORY W. MEEKS, New York
STEVE CHABOT, Ohio	ALBIO SIRES, New Jersey
JOE WILSON, South Carolina	GERALD E. CONNOLLY, Virginia
MICHAEL T. McCAUL, Texas	THEODORE E. DEUTCH, Florida
TED POE, Texas	BRIAN HIGGINS, New York
MATT SALMON, Arizona	KAREN BASS, California
DARRELL E. ISSA, California	WILLIAM KEATING, Massachusetts
TOM MARINO, Pennsylvania	DAVID CICILLINE, Rhode Island
JEFF DUNCAN, South Carolina	ALAN GRAYSON, Florida
MO BROOKS, Alabama	AMI BERA, California
PAUL COOK, California	ALAN S. LOWENTHAL, California
RANDY K. WEBER SR., Texas	GRACE MENG, New York
SCOTT PERRY, Pennsylvania	LOIS FRANKEL, Florida
RON DeSANTIS, Florida	TULSI GABBARD, Hawaii
MARK MEADOWS, North Carolina	JOAQUIN CASTRO, Texas
TED S. YOHO, Florida	ROBIN L. KELLY, Illinois
CURT CLAWSON, Florida	BRENDAN F. BOYLE, Pennsylvania
SCOTT DesJARLAIS, Tennessee	
REID J. RIBBLE, Wisconsin	
DAVID A. TROTT, Michigan	
LEE M. ZELDIN, New York	
TOM EMMER, Minnesota	

AMY PORTER, *Chief of Staff*   THOMAS SHEEHY, *Staff Director*

JASON STEINBAUM, *Democratic Staff Director*

SUBCOMMITTEE ON TERRORISM, NONPROLIFERATION, AND TRADE

TED POE, Texas, *Chairman*

JOE WILSON, South Carolina	WILLIAM KEATING, Massachusetts
DARRELL E. ISSA, California	BRAD SHERMAN, California
PAUL COOK, California	BRIAN HIGGINS, New York
SCOTT PERRY, Pennsylvania	JOAQUIN CASTRO, Texas
REID J. RIBBLE, Wisconsin	ROBIN L. KELLY, Illinois
LEE M. ZELDIN, New York	

CONTENTS

———

POACHING AND TERRORISM: A NATIONAL SECURITY CHALLENGE

WEDNESDAY, APRIL 22, 2015

House of Representatives,
Subcommittee on Terrorism, Nonproliferation, and Trade,
Committee on Foreign Affairs,
Washington, DC.

The subcommittee met, pursuant to notice, at 3 o'clock p.m., in room 2172, Rayburn House Office Building, Hon. Ted Poe (chairman of the subcommittee) presiding.

Mr. Poe. The subcommittee will come to order.

Without objection, all members may have 5 days to submit statements, questions, and extraneous materials for the record subject to the length limitations in the rules.

I will proceed with my opening statement. Elephant and rhino populations in Africa are being decimated by poachers looking for high profits with little risk and little consequences. Between 1990 and 2005, poachers killed an average of 14 rhinos each year in South Africa. In 2013 and again in 2014, they killed over 1,000 rhinos each year. The black rhino population has declined by 93 percent since the 1960s. A total of only five white rhinos are left in the whole world today. Elephants are in just as much trouble. And I have a slide, and members of the panel also have this poster in front of you somewhere that you can refer to.

As you can see from this map by National Geographic, there were approximately 1.3 million elephants in Africa in 1979. The light brown areas are where elephants roamed in 1979. The dark brown areas are where they roamed in 2007. The dark brown areas are just a fraction of the light brown areas. We see that the elephants and their population are being diminished considerably.

I also have a poster here of Satao, the elephant. Some say he was the oldest elephant in Africa. We don't know. His tusks were so long that they hit the ground before poachers got to him and killed him for the tusk and left the rest of him in Africa.

The elephant population has dropped 60 percent since 1979, and poaching numbers rise. Why? It is all about the money. The black market price of ivory in Africa is anywhere between $1,000 and $1,800 per pound. A rhino horn is now worth about $60,000 per kilogram. That is 2.2 pounds. That is twice the value of gold and platinum and more than cocaine or diamonds. In all, the illegal wildlife trade is estimated as a $10 billion to $20 billion a year business. With all the money, it is no surprise that poachers are using more advanced weaponry that leaves park rangers looking like Little Bo Peep trying to fight against Arnold Schwarzenegger. Poachers can now swoop down in the dead of night in helicopters, with high-powered rifles. Even if the traffickers are caught and convicted, the penalties are far less than if the traffickers were convicted of crimes in drug trafficking. Punishments in most countries are little more than a slap on the wrist or none at all. Low risk and high profits make for a deadly combination.

Demand is being driven mainly from the Asian countries. Once again, there is a slide in front of our panelists, and it is on the monitor for those in the audience. This map is from an NGO called TRAFFIC. The main ivory seizures follow trade routes from Africa to Asia. Ivory is shipped out in places like Tanzania, Kenya, and South Africa; trafficked through the Philippines and Malaysia; and ends up in Thailand and, yes, China as well.

Vietnam is the largest consumer of rhino horns that are poached. Users there believe the rhino horn can cure everything from cancer to hangovers. Many see it as a status symbol. I understand the rhino horn is ground down into a powder and put in different products and is sold at an expensive rate. People want it because there is a demand. They believe there is some magic, so to speak, or benefit from the rhino horn powder.

Criminals and thugs are not the only bad actors involved in this dirty business, and that is what this hearing is about today. Terrorist groups, such as Al Qaeda affiliate Al Shabaab, Boko Haram, the LRA, and others, are all involved in poaching. We do not know to what extent these groups are involved, how much money they make off of poaching, or their interactions with criminal and smuggling groups. We can't solve the problem if we don't understand it.

The intelligence community needs to commit more resources to understand this problem. The Obama administration released a strategy to combat wildlife trafficking in 2014, February. It took another year to develop an implementation plan to execute the strategy. The strategy and the implementation plan are important steps in the right direction, but we need to do a whole lot more.

While there are sections devoted to measuring progress, nowhere in the plan is there a commitment to rigorous evaluations. Impact of those evaluations are the only way that we can know if our programs are working. Nor is there a timeline mentioned anywhere in the plan.

The Achilles' heel of the implementation plan could be its lack of dedicated resources. The administration needs to have a cross-cutting budget that will outline exactly how much money we are spending on anti-poaching efforts.

There are other steps we can take. One easy step is to increase the penalty for those caught trafficking wildlife so as not to let them come into the United States. A consular official should be able to reject a visa for those that have been convicted of wildlife trafficking. The Treasury Department should aggressively sanction wildlife traffickers. This does not need to be an act of Congress. The administration has the authority to do this.

The problem is so bad that those in Africa that are trying to enforce the law have very little resources. They are unarmed. Several of the rangers that work in these national parks are murdered each year. The bad guys have, as I mentioned, helicopters, automatic weapons. They shoot these animals from the air, and there is very little defense against them that is being taking place in my opinion.

We need to empower law enforcement. Right now a drug trafficker's profit is going to help a designated foreign terrorist organization, and our law enforcement can go after the drug trafficker regardless of whether or not there is a nexus back to the U.S. We now know wildlife trafficking money goes to help terrorists, like the drug money does. We should change U.S. Law so law enforcement can go after wildlife traffickers just like it can go after international drug traffickers.

Strengthening law enforcement and reducing demand is a solution to this problem, but it will not be quick. If we don't act, terrorists will keep taxiing in big profits while driving elephants and rhinos into extinction. Meanwhile, they find money to further their terrorist enterprises throughout the world.

I will now yield to the ranking member. I didn't say Yankee member. I said ranking member.

Mr. KEATING. As long you didn't say Yankee member.

Mr. POE. For his opening statement.

Mr. KEATING. Thank you, Mr. Chairman, and thank you for conducting this hearing.

I would also like to thank our witnesses for being here today. It is important we have each of the co-chairs of the President's Task Force on Combating Wildlife Trafficking this afternoon. We understand your schedule is in very high demand, and we appreciate your willingness to accommodate this important hearing. As we honor Earth Day today, it is particularly timely that this afternoon's hearing will discuss an integral facet of international conservation effects.

Illicit trade in wildlife is a serious global environmental crime with significant negative impacts for endangered species protection, ecosystem stability, and biodiversity conservation. Unfortunately, this problem is only growing. It is estimated that illegal wildlife trafficking is the fourth largest global illegal activity after only narcotics, counterfeiting, and human trafficking.

Of particular concern is the rise in demand for products from illegally poached animals, particularly from elephants and rhinoceroses in China, Vietnam, and other destination countries. This has dramatically increased the prices and led to a rapid expansion of illicit markets. In fact, this illegal trade is believed to have more than doubled since 2007. The black market price of rhino horn is over $30,000 per pound, more than the value of platinum, and poaching is bringing rhinoceroses to the edge of extinction.

Wildlife trafficking is also a real and increasing threat to our national security. Ivory like so many blood diamonds, is funding many armed fighters in Africa. Reports indicate that terrorists and militant groups—such as Al Shabaab in Somalia; the Lord's Resistance Army (LRA) in Central Africa; and Janjaweed in Sudan and Chad—are involved in poaching elephants and dealing in ivory. There are also reports that militants affiliated with Al Qaeda are involved in the illegal trade of ivory, tiger pelts, and rhino horns in India, Nepal, Burma, and Thailand.

Further, much of the global illegal trade in wildlife is run by transitional criminal organizations, which are attracted to wildlife trafficking because of its low risk of detection, high profits, and weak penalties. These organized criminal groups often use smuggling routes, money-laundering schemes, and other techniques similar to those of drug traffickers.

According to the U.S. intelligence community, the illicit ivory and rhino horn trade is enabled by official corruption in many source countries which undermines the rule of law and contributes to border instability. There are even reported instances where government military forces are directly involved in poaching and wildlife trafficking, such as in the Democratic Republic of the Congo, South Sudan, Tanzania, Uganda, and Zimbabwe. And it is important that we do not overlook the role of illegal, unreported, and unregulated fishing, including shark finning and how that plays to the condition, and how it surrounds additional illicit activity, including piracy, smuggling, and illegal trafficking of weapons and people. Each year it is estimated that 100 million sharks are killed, and stripped of their fins, to meet demand for shark fin soup, a delicacy in fine menus across China.

Indeed, these activities are inexorably linked with illegal fishing activities often supported by forced labor and human trafficking of migrant traffickers and children, both in the oceans and the Great Lakes region in Africa. The United States needs to know more about these links between militant groups, transnational organized crime, and corrupt state actors in the illegal wildlife trade.

In responding to this growing environmental and national security threat, I am encouraging the administration's recent implementation plan giving effect of the National Security Strategy for Combating Wildlife Trafficking. I look forward to learning more today about our progress and meeting the objectives of this implementation plan, particularly with respect to efforts to assist our international partners in strengthening global enforcement and reducing demand for illegally traded wildlife.

I also look forward to an update on the potential changes to the U.S. Fish and Wildlife Service regulations and further restrictions surrounding ivory trade within the United States and whether these regulations will provide clarity for antiques and other proper commercial and educational uses of ivory.

Thank you, again, Mr. Chairman, and I yield back.

Mr. POE. I thank the gentleman for his opening statement.

I want to introduce into the record an article that was written today in Business Insider by Gretchen Peters and Juan Zarate.

[The information referred to follows:]

How financial power can be used to save iconic species from extinction

Business Insider
Gretchen Peters and Juan Zarate, Contributor
Apr. 22, 2015, 1:44 PM

Thomas Mukoya/ReutersA Kenya Wildlife Services ranger shows elephant tusks intercepted from poachers during a commemoration of the 1989 ivory burning at the Nairobi National Park on July 18, 2009.

On Earth Day 2015, prospects for many of the planet's most iconic species look bleak

Unless poaching rates decline across Africa, the rhino and elephant will be extinct within a decade. The world has lost 97% of its tigers in the last 50 years, and the great apes are on pace to disappear within a generation.

This is not just a conservation tragedy. It's also a national security crisis.

Wildlife trafficking is a big business that's fueling conflict and terror. The United Nations Office on Drugs and Crime (UNODC) has estimated that wildlife trafficking, forestry and other environmental crime nets approximately $8 to $10 billion USD annually.

Smuggling wildlife is as profitable as trafficking in humans, arms, and drugs.

A myriad of powerful, violent groups, including organized crime syndicates, insurgent and terror networks, are industrializing this trade to both profit and foment conflict. They often collude with corrupt officials and businesses along the supply chain.

The Lord's Resistance Army (LRA), known for child abduction, sex slavery, and the use of child soldiers, is involved in elephant poaching. In 2011, LRA's leader, Joseph Kony, ordered members to increase ivory trafficking to sustain the group.

The Sudanese Janjaweed, notorious for their atrocities in Darfur, have profited from the ivory trade. Since the September 2013 Westgate mall attack, there have also been reports that Al Qaeda's Africa affiliate, Al Shabaab, is acting as a middleman for the ivory trade. Slaughtering elephants is fueling crimes against humanity.

Networks of organized criminals and shadowy syndicates form part of the business chain, facilitating and financing illicit wildlife trade from Africa to Asia. Powerful Chinese triads, South Asian drug traffickers — some with direct links to terror networks — and Southeast Asian wildlife traders all take part. "Untouchable" smugglers, like Vixay Keosavang, known as the "Pablo Escobar of wildlife crime" smuggle everything from rhino horn to pangolin scales to lion bones.

Recognizing the need to combat wildlife trafficking, President Obama issued an Executive Order in 2013 along with a national strategy in 2014. As a result, there have been efforts to improve US law, increase budgets to combat wildlife trafficking, and post additional US officers abroad to interdict such trade.

These are important steps. But they are not enough.

APFighters from Somali al Qaeda affiliate Al Shabaab — beneficiaries of illegal wildlife trafficking.

Authorities scrambling to implement these new US policies are confronted with major challenges. Penalties for wildlife traffickers remain weak or non-existent around the globe; powerful syndicate leaders are politically protected; and well-armed and funded networks have governments outgunned, outspent and often corrupted.

This conservation crisis has not been treated as the global security threat it is. There is an opportunity to galvanize action to save endangered species while targeting groups that profit from this trade and fuel conflict.

We can leverage the financial pressure playbook the United States has used effectively since the September 11th attacks to target terrorist financiers, proliferation, and problematic state actors like Iran.

President Obama should sign a new Executive Order authorizing the use of targeted sanctions that empower the US Treasury to identify and isolate those involved in the illicit wildlife trade.

A regime of "Earth Sanctions," designed to target the assets of individuals, front companies, shippers, regimes, and illicit networks sabotaging our planet's resources and threatening our national security would provide an essential tool to fight and deter the wildlife trade. At the same time, they could help disrupt a source of revenue for some of the most dangerous terrorist and militia groups.

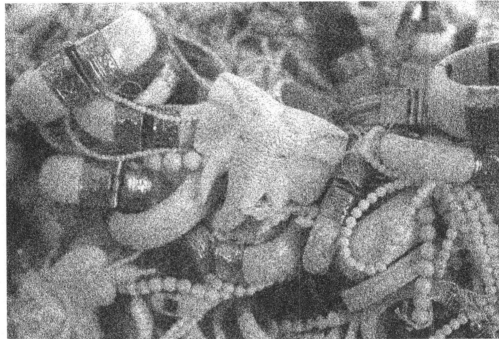

Rick Wilking/ReutersConfiscated ivory jewelry is displayed before the U.S. Fish and Wildlife Service crushed 6 tons of ivory, in Denver, Colorado on November 14, 2013.

For this to be effective, there would need to be a small, dedicated group of analysts, investigators, and prosecutors dedicated to mapping, tracking, and targeting the assets held by the transnational syndicates trading in wildlife.

Such a sanctions package would build on the targeted regimes that already focus on illicit transnational activity, like drug trafficking and organized crime. It would be effective against those who most need access to the formal banking and commercial system to trade and do business.

Given the effect of such measures globally, this type of financial isolation reaches well beyond US ports and borders. Chinese triads trafficking rhino horn from South Africa to Asia could be targeted, with their financial access and interests put at risk.

The US government could sanction unscrupulous timber and mining firms in Congo and Gabon that smuggle ivory under the cover of their "legitimate" business operations. Corrupt senior officials and military leaders who protect and facilitate the wildlife trade in Tanzania, Kenya, Sudan and Cameroon could be blocked from the global financial system and from travel to the United States.

Earth Sanctions would widen opportunities to target those financially facilitating sanctioned groups, such as Al-Shabaab in Somalia and the Lord's Resistance Army. They could also deter those deciding whether to enter the market.

Such sanctions would put a greater onus on the private sector implicated in this trade — which includes banks, port management companies, maritime shipping firms and airlines — to ensure they are not unwittingly facilitating the illicit traffic of endangered species.

Michał Huniewicz (Elephants) [CC-BY-2.0], via Wikimedia Commons and by U.S. Fish and Wildlife Service Headquarters

But solving the problem requires an even broader international framework. The US should propose a new UN sanctions regime to parallel the Executive Order, putting pressure on China to work cooperatively to stem demand, address corruption, and assist with interdiction. There are signs that even Beijing recognizes that the networks smuggling ivory and rhino horn are more than just a threat to conservation.

The Financial Action Task Force (FATF) should concentrate on identifying typologies of wildlife trafficking, developing standards, and assessing countries on how to effectively prevent the financing and laundering of proceeds of this trade.

The Egmont Group of financial intelligence units — especially those based in Africa — could target collection tied to wildlife trafficking networks and financing, and groups like Interpol, the World Customs Organization, and the private sector could amplify their focus on gathering data regarding major poachers and transnational criminal networks.

Coupled with important publicity campaigns to build consumer awareness led by celebrities like Yao Ming, Kathryn Bigelow, Prince William, and David Beckham, these efforts could build a coalition to save these iconic species while simultaneously undermining poachers, organized criminals, militants, and terrorists.

This year's Earth Day is a moment to commit to our collective natural and national security. Time is running out.

Gretchen Peters is an advisor to Parcs Gabon on wildlife trafficking, the senior fellow on transnational crime at the Terrorism, Transnational Crime and Corruption CENTER, and Executive Director of the Satao Project.

Juan Zarate is the former deputy national security advisor for combatting terrorism and assistant secretary of the Treasury for terrorist financing and financial crimes. They are both members of the Board of Advisors to the Center on Sanctions and Illicit Finance at the Foundation for Defense of Democracies.

You probably know these individuals. I will just read two short sentences: On Earth Day 2015, prospects for many of the planet's most iconic species are bleak. Unless poaching rates deadline across Africa, the rhino and elephant will be extinct within a decade. The world has lost 97 percent of its tigers in the last 50 years, and the great apes are on the pace to disappear within a generation. It is a national security crisis.

Anyway, I will now introduce our three experts: Ambassador Judith Garber is Acting Assistant Secretary for the Bureau of Oceans and International Environmental and Scientific Affairs at the Department of State. Ambassador Garber has held diplomatic positions all over the world, including serving as the U.S. Ambassador to Latvia.

Robert Dreher is Associate Director of the U.S. Fish and Wildlife Service at the Department of the Interior. Before joining the Fish and Wildlife, Mr. Dreher served as acting assistant attorney general for the Environment and Natural Resources Division of the Department of Justice.

Mr. John Cruden is the new Acting Assistant Attorney General for the Environmental and Natural Resources Division at the Department of Justice. Mr. Cruden has a long history of public service at the Department of Justice and in the military.

Ambassador Garber, we will start with you for your opening statement of 5 minutes.

STATEMENT OF THE HONORABLE JUDITH G. GARBER, ACTING ASSISTANT SECRETARY, BUREAU OF OCEANS AND INTERNATIONAL AND ENVIRONMENTAL AND SCIENTIFIC AFFAIRS, U.S. DEPARTMENT OF STATE

Ambassador GARBER. Thank you, Mr. Chairman.

Good afternoon, Chairman Poe and Ranking Member Keating. I greatly appreciate the opportunity to appear before you today. With your permission, I would like to submit my written statement for the record.

Mr. POE. Without objection, it will be made a part of the record.

Ambassador GARBER. At the outset, let me extend my thanks to the subcommittee for holding this hearing today, which marks the 45th anniversary of Earth Day. Events are being planned today in the United States and around the world, including by our missions overseas to raise awareness and concern for the environment, including wildlife. Wildlife trafficking is a multi-billion-dollar criminal enterprise that poses a serious and urgent threat to conservation and national security. The increasing involvement of armed groups and criminal elements of all kinds, including some terrorist entities, threatens the peace and security of fragile regions, strengthens illicit trade routes, and destabilizes economies and communities that depend on wildlife for their livelihoods.

Recognizing the scale and seriousness of this problem, I am determined that the United States should be part of the solution. President Obama issued an Executive order that established an interagency task force co-chaired by the Departments of State, Justice and Interior, and charged it with developing a strategy to guide U.S. efforts. The resulting National Strategy for Combating Wildlife Trafficking fortifies U.S. leadership on countering the global security threat posed by wildlife trafficking. It directs our efforts to, one, strengthen domestic and global enforcement; two, reduce demand at home and abroad; and, three, build international commitment, cooperation, and public-private partnerships to combat wildlife trafficking.

As you both noted, the task force has also developed an implementation plan for the strategy. Released in February, the plan is our road map going forward. It lays out specific next steps, identifies lead agencies for each objective, and defines how we will measure our progress. The plan demonstrates that we are in this for the long haul.

Our work over the past year has been intensive. I will just highlight a few of the key actions the Department of State has taken. We are expanding our existing efforts to improve cross-border law enforcement cooperation, strengthen wildlife trafficking legislation, and enhance wildlife management. We are providing critical training to park rangers, police, custom officials, prosecutors, and judges. For example, the Department recently supported INTERPOL police investigative training in Vietnam, a key demand country.

The strategy also recognizes that we must address demand that is driving poaching to unprecedented levels. We must raise awareness about the devastating impacts of wildlife trafficking. To this end, we are working closely with NGOs, many of whom have ongoing public outreach campaigns, as well as the private sector. For example, we are providing over $37,000 to support the NGO WildAid for its African Wildlife Pride campaign to focus on the urgent need to stop poaching. We are continuing to catalyze political will and action by highlighting wildlife trafficking in multilateral fora.

Last year we were able to include language addressing trafficking in two Security Council resolutions sanctioning African armed groups. In December, at a conference in Tanzania, Under Secretary Novelli jump started regional cooperation in East Africa to address the poaching crisis.

We have made significant progress in interactions with China. Last July, during the U.S.-China Strategic and Economic Dialogue, Secretary Kerry and China's Vice Premier Liu confirmed their commitment to stamp out illegal trade in wildlife. In November, President Obama and President Xi reaffirmed this commitment and agreed to cooperate in the areas of e-commerce, public outreach, joint training, and law enforcement. Last month I met with Chinese officials in Beijing to push these issues forward, as well as with Chinese wildlife NGOs who expressed appreciation for our attention to these issues.

Moving forward, we are also leveraging trade agreements to press countries and regions which account for a sizeable portion of the illegal trade in wildlife to live up to their commitments to combat wildlife trafficking and strengthen wildlife conservation. Indeed, the administration is pursuing such obligations in the Trans-Pacific Partnership Agreement with 11 other countries in the Asia-Pacific region, as well as the Transatlantic Partnership Agreement negotiations with the European Union. These commitments will be fully enforceable, including through recourse to trade sanctions, which will be a powerful incentive for parties to match words with actions.

In closing, let me just say that we are working across the U.S. Government to focus our international investments to combat wildlife trafficking in the most strategic and effective way possible. Congress has shown great leadership on this issue, and we truly appreciate your support. We look forward to working closely with you in our continuing efforts to stop this global scourge.

I appreciate the opportunity to appear before you today, and I will be happy to answer any questions you may have. Thank you.

[The prepared statement of Ms. Garber follows:]

Statement of
Judith G. Garber
Acting Assistant Secretary of State
Bureau of Oceans and International Environmental and
Scientific Affairs
U.S. Department of State

Before the Subcommittee on Terrorism, Nonproliferation and Trade
Committee on Foreign Affairs
U.S. House of Representatives

April 22, 2015

Introduction

Good afternoon Chairman Poe, Ranking Member Keating, and other Members of the Terrorism, Nonproliferation, and Trade Subcommittee of the House Committee on Foreign Affairs. I appreciate the opportunity to appear before you today.

It's particularly fitting that we are holding this hearing today, which marks the 45th anniversary of Earth Day. As you well know, events are being held around the world today to raise public awareness and concern for organisms, the environment and public health. Wildlife trafficking threatens each of these areas: iconic species are being pushed to the brink of extinction; illegal harvest of and trade in plants and trees destroys needed habitat and opens access to previously remote populations of highly endangered wildlife; and the illegal trade in live animals and their parts bypasses public health controls and puts human populations at risk for disease.

Wildlife trafficking is a multi-billion-dollar criminal enterprise that is both a conservation concern and an acute security threat. The increasing involvement of organized crime in poaching and trafficking of wildlife promotes corruption, threatens peace and security of fragile regions, strengthens illicit trade routes, destabilizes economies and communities that depend on wildlife for their livelihoods, and contributes to the spread of disease.

The good news is that the international community is coming together in an unprecedented way to combat this pernicious trade. Shared understanding and commitment, along with the efforts of governments, the international community, intergovernmental organizations, NGOs, corporations, civil society, and individuals are critical for collective action to address this evolving transnational threat.

The State Department has long recognized the threats that wildlife trafficking poses and Secretary Kerry has long championed efforts to combat wildlife trafficking. As Chairman of the Senate Foreign Relations Committee, he held hearings on the subject. In his role as Secretary of State, he has called on leaders everywhere to step up and meet the challenge of stopping the trade in illegal wildlife products across the supply chain from source to consumer.

National Strategy

Recognizing the urgent need for a coordinated response to this growing global crisis, on July 1, 2013, President Obama issued an Executive Order that established an inter-agency Task Force on combating wildlife trafficking co-chaired by the Departments of State, Justice, and the Interior and charged it with developing a strategy to guide U.S. efforts on this issue. The *National Strategy for Combating Wildlife Trafficking* (National Strategy) was released on February 11, 2014, and describes a "whole of government" approach to tackle this growing threat, identifying priority areas for inter-agency coordination, with the objectives of harnessing and strategically applying the full breadth of federal resources. The National Strategy further strengthens U.S. leadership on countering the global security threat posed by transnational criminal organizations that engage in illegal trade in wildlife. It sets three strategic priorities:

- Strengthening domestic and global enforcement, including assessing the related laws, regulations, and enforcement tools;

- Reducing demand for illegally traded wildlife at home and abroad; and

- Building international cooperation and public-private partnerships to combat wildlife poaching and illegal trade.

Implementation Plan

Recognizing that this issue will require significant and sustained effort, over the past year, the Bureau of Oceans and International Environmental and Scientific Affairs (OES) worked closely with the Co-chairs and other members of the Task Force to develop an Implementation Plan for the National Strategy. The Implementation Plan was released this past February on the first anniversary of the release of the National Strategy. The Plan will be our roadmap going forward; it details how we will further realize the Strategy's goals, laying out specific next steps, identifying lead agencies for each objective, and defining how we will measure our progress.

Over the past year, as we were developing the Plan, work in the three strategic priority areas has been intensive. OES is leading coordination of two elements of the Strategy – the international cooperation and partnerships and demand reduction components, and – through our support for regional Wildlife Enforcement Networks (WENs) – contributing to the global enforcement element as well.

Strengthening Domestic and Global Enforcement

Driven by high demand and high profits for wildlife and wildlife products, coupled with low risk of detection and often inadequate penalties, criminal syndicates are increasingly drawn to wildlife trafficking, which generates revenues conservatively estimated at $8-10 billion per year. Rhino horn, for example, is currently worth more than gold, yet in many parts of the world those caught engaging in wildlife trafficking may risk small fines or minimal jail sentencing.

The National Strategy recognizes that to combat wildlife trafficking effectively, countries need to have strong investigative, enforcement, and judicial capabilities in order to respond to wildlife crime, combat corruption, and disrupt trafficking networks and bring traffickers to justice. To this end, under the leadership of the State Department's Bureau of International Narcotics and Law Enforcement Affairs, we are expanding on our existing international efforts to improve cross-border law enforcement cooperation, strengthen wildlife trafficking legislation, enhance wildlife management, and provide critical training to park rangers, police, customs officials, prosecutors, and judges.

The State Department is working to build global law enforcement capacity in Africa, East Asia and the Pacific, and Latin America. The International Law Enforcement Academy (ILEA) Program will continue to provide regional wildlife investigative training at ILEAs in Bangkok and Gaborone. Since 2002, the State Department has trained over 450 law enforcement officers in investigating wildlife crime through Fish and Wildlife Service instruction at ILEA Gaborone.

Together with the United States Agency for International Development (USAID), the United States Fish and Wildlife Service (USFWS), and international partners, the State Department funded Cobra II, a global cooperative effort to combat wildlife trafficking from December 2013 through January 2014. The month-long operation brought together police, customs, and wildlife officials from 28 countries, including China, the United States, and African and Southeast Asian nations, with international enforcement agencies. Together they conducted investigations out of two main coordination centers in Nairobi and Bangkok, with links to field operatives across Africa and Asia. The cross-border law enforcement cooperation and enhanced capacity resulted in numerous arrests of wildlife criminals and significant wildlife seizures across Africa and Asia.

To increase international police and customs investigative capability, the State Department has funded advanced wildlife investigations courses in Thailand organized by U.S. Immigration and Customs Enforcement, Homeland Security Investigations (ICE /HSI). Furthermore the State Department recently approved funding for an ICE /HSI Transnational Criminal Investigations Unit in Nairobi, Kenya, whose mission will include investigating wildlife trafficking.

Wildlife Enforcement Networks (WENs)

For the last decade, the State Department and USAID have worked with our partners inside the federal government and external partners to build active coordination and improve information sharing by supporting the establishment of Wildlife Enforcement Networks (WENs) in Southeast Asia, South Asia, Central America, the Horn of Africa, and Southern Africa. The State Department is supporting efforts to develop WENs in Southern Africa, South America and the Caribbean. USAID is continuing its investments in the South Asia WEN, while the Southeast Asian WEN is becoming increasingly integrated into the Association of Southeast Asian Nations and serving as a model for other WENs such as that in Southern Africa.

As we work to establish more regional networks, we are also working with the International Consortium to Combat Wildlife Crime and other partners to support the creation of a global network of regional WENs to improve communication and strengthen response actions across enforcement agencies globally. By the end of this year, USFWS is also planning to station law enforcement agents at key U.S. missions in Africa, Asia, and South America to partner with and assist law enforcement entities.

National Security

We are increasingly concerned with links to terrorists and rogue security personnel. There is evidence that some insurgent groups are directly involved in poaching or trafficking, who then trade wildlife products for weapons or safe haven. Like many illicit activities, it is difficult to determine the extent to which these actors are involved in wildlife trafficking. We believe that, at a minimum, these groups are likely sharing some of the same facilitators – such as corrupt customs and border officials, money launderers, and supply chains.

We still have much to learn about the full extent of terrorists and militant groups involvement with wildlife trafficking. One of the goals of our assistance efforts is to promote greater information sharing and coordination within and among governments, law enforcement and intelligence agencies, conservation groups and other actors working in this area.

Reducing Demand for Illegally Traded Wildlife

Global demand for wildlife products has soared in recent years, resulting in a dramatic increase in poaching. The Central African forest elephant population declined by approximately two-thirds between 2002 and 2011, putting forest elephants on track for extinction within the next decade. In 2014, 1,215 rhinos were poached in South Africa alone. At this rate, more than three rhinos are killed *per day* for their horns. This is up from just thirteen rhinos poached in the entire year in 2007.

The National Strategy recognizes that we must address the demand that is driving poaching to unprecedented levels. We recognize that reducing demand is a complex and long-term endeavor, and effective strategies will be species- and country- specific.

Our demand reduction activities include support for campaigns to raise awareness about the devastating impacts of wildlife poaching and trafficking. A significant effort to reduce demand specifically in Asia is the USAID-funded Asia's Regional Response to Endangered Species Trafficking (ARREST) program. The ARREST program, which USAID plans to support through 2016, has launched a series of strategically targeted, government-endorsed demand reduction campaigns in Thailand, Vietnam, and China and has already been successful in reducing demand for shark fins.

At the State Department, we are engaging diplomatically to catalyze political will and mobilize global support for the fight against wildlife trafficking. This includes efforts to strengthen international agreements that protect wildlife, promote conservation commitments, and fight wildlife trafficking within and between countries and regions, while enlisting the support of our partners – ranging from non-profit conservation groups and grass-roots activists to private industry and the media.

During the July 2014 U.S.-China Strategic and Economic Dialogue (S&ED) in Beijing Secretary Kerry participated in a public event on wildlife trafficking with China's Vice Premier Liu, State Councilor Yang, and Chinese basketball star Yao Ming. At the event, Secretary Kerry, Liu and Yang reconfirmed their commitment to stamp out the illegal trade in wildlife and wildlife products and called for greater international cooperation to address the issue. President Obama and Chinese President Xi Jinping reaffirmed this commitment last November when they met in Beijing. There they pledged to work together to stop the trade in illegal wildlife products across the supply chain from source to consumer through work in the areas of e-commerce, public outreach, joint training, and law enforcement. During the S&ED we also agreed to a session on wildlife trafficking again at the 7th S&ED, to be held this June here in Washington.

As we move forward, we will apply the lessons learned from past campaigns, such as what messages and activities are effective in certain regions. We will also draw from the expertise of the NGO community and the private sector, including the transportation and tourism sectors and online retailers, as we develop a more comprehensive demand reduction strategy.

Building International Cooperation and Public-Private Partnerships

Wildlife trafficking is a global challenge that requires a global response. The National Strategy recognizes that combating wildlife trafficking requires the engagement of governments in range, transit, and demand countries worldwide, and we must use diplomacy to catalyze political will.

One such way is by leveraging trade agreements and trade policy to press countries and regions which account for a sizeable portion of the consumption, illegal take and trade of wildlife and wildlife products to uphold their commitments to combat wildlife trafficking and strengthen wildlife conservation. Indeed, the Administration is pursuing such obligations in the Trans-Pacific Partnership Agreement (TPP) with eleven other countries in the Asia-Pacific region accounting for an estimated $ 8-10 billion in illegal wildlife trade, as well as the Transatlantic Partnership Agreement (T-TIP) negotiations with the European Union (EU).

These commitments would be fully enforceable, including through recourse to trade sanctions, which will be a powerful incentive for parties to match words with action.

We have also advocated for countries to work together against wildlife trafficking in a number of multilateral fora, including the Asia Pacific Economic Cooperation forum, or APEC, the Association of Southeast Asian Nations, or ASEAN, the G-7, the UN General Assembly, the UN Office on Drugs and Crime, and the UN Commission on Crime Prevention and Criminal Justice. We have also pressed the African Union, the African Development Bank, and multiple Regional Economic Communities in Africa to mobilize efforts to combat wildlife trafficking. We worked with our mission to the U.N. to secure the inclusion of language to address wildlife trafficking in two Security Council Resolutions sanctioning African armed groups, which were adopted in January 2014. APEC has committed to addressing wildlife trafficking in Declarations for the last three years, and in 2014 and 2015 is conducting follow-on programming, with State Department support, to build capacity in the region to reduce demand and strengthen enforcement. The 2014 East Asia Summit, attended by the United States, ASEAN, and other nations, produced a Declaration on Combating Wildlife Trafficking focused on strengthening regional enforcement cooperation and upholding commitments under the Convention on International Trade in Endangered Species of Wild Fauna and Flora.

We are expanding our efforts to raise wildlife trafficking at all levels of our bilateral diplomatic and development engagement with foreign governments. U.S. Ambassadors and USAID Mission Directors in African countries and other State Department and USAID principals have encouraged high-level African government officials to take concrete steps to protect their wildlife, prevent trafficking and the corruption it breeds, and promote opportunity and development for communities. Building on these efforts, the Secretary of the Interior hosted a U.S.-Africa Leaders Summit Signature Event, a *Dialogue on Combating Wildlife Trafficking*, on August 4, 2014, which convened key African heads of state and foreign ministers to elevate wildlife conservation as a national priority and encourage African leadership and regional collaboration as essential components for efforts to stop poaching and trafficking at the source.

Conclusion

Combating wildlife trafficking is a complex challenge which demands a multi-faceted and whole-of-government approach. Within the framework of the National

Strategy and the Implementation Plan, we are working across the U.S. Government to focus our international investments to combat wildlife trafficking in the most strategic and effective way possible.

We appreciate your support and interest essential to our efforts. I would be pleased to answer any questions that you may have.

———————

Mr. POE. Thank you, Ambassador.

Mr. Dreher, we will hear your opening statement.

STATEMENT OF MR. ROBERT DREHER, ASSOCIATE DIRECTOR, U.S. FISH AND WILDLIFE SERVICE, U.S. DEPARTMENT OF THE INTERIOR

Mr. DREHER. All right. So I lost 5 seconds without a microphone. I am sorry.

Good afternoon, Mr. Chairman and Ranking Member Keating, and members of the subcommittee. I am Bob Dreher, Associate Director of the U.S. Fish and Wildlife Service.

I appreciate the opportunity to be here today, on Earth Day fittingly, to discuss the current wildlife trafficking crisis that threatens to wipe out the African elephant, rhinoceros, and a host of other species around the globe. As you noted, elephants are being slaughtered for ivory today at unprecedented rates, and the poaching of rhinos for their horns has surged upward.

Wildlife trafficking once was predominantly a crime of opportunity committed by local individuals or small groups. Today it increasingly involves highly organized criminal networks capable of moving large commercial volumes of illegal wildlife products. Through our law enforcement investigations, we have seen direct links between wildlife trafficking and organized crime. My written testimony highlights some of our work disrupting large-scale wildlife trafficking networks: Operation Crash, for example, an ongoing nationwide criminal investigation led by the service that focuses on U.S. involvement in the black market for rhino horn and elephant ivory.

I wanted to give the subcommittee members a more graphic sense of what is happening, and I have some slides. The first two are photos illustrating the brutal slaughter of elephants and rhinos. And we have seen these pictures before.

What I want to point out is that this sort of wanton killing is no longer just the action of local individuals. It is increasingly the work of organized criminal networks who send heavily armed teams into protected areas with commissions to take elephant ivory or rhino horn, who organize the shipping of the still-bloody ivory and rhino horns through international channels, and who deliver these highly valuable products to buyers in undercover markets ranging from East Asia to the United States.

Photo 3, to give you a sense of the scale of these operations, these photos show the evidence seized in 1 day in one of our Operation Crash cases from safety deposit boxes, residences, and businesses in the United States in southern California: Over $1 million in cash, $1 million in gold, as well as rhino horns, and other wildlife parts.

The next three slides just show a number of the individuals and businesses convicted here in the United States as part of Operation Crash. What I think you can see is that what was once a local or regional problem has become a global crisis, as increasingly sophisticated, violent, and ruthless criminal organizations have branched into wildlife trafficking.

To address this escalating wildlife trafficking crisis, the Service is building on decades of its work to increase our efforts in our Office of Law Enforcement and our International Affairs Programs. We are working across the U.S. Government to take a coordinated approach. In February, the White House released the implementation plan for the National Strategy for Combating Wildlife Trafficking. The implementation plan reaffirms our Nation's commitment to work in partnership with governments, local communities, nongovernmental organizations, and the private sector, to address wildlife trafficking.

We took an enormous step forward in 2013 when the United States destroyed its 6-ton stock of confiscated elephant ivory, sending a clear message we will not tolerate wildlife crime. Several other governments have since followed suit, and we now are in a much better position to work with the international community to crack down on poaching and illegal wildlife trade.

I would also like to commend Congress for passing legislation last year to reauthorize the Save Vanishing Species stamp. Since the stamp's inception in 2011, more than 26 million stamps have been purchased by the American public, generating more than $2.6 million for conservation of elephants, rhinos, tigers, great apes, and marine turtles.

With assistance from the State Department, we have begun stationing Service law enforcement agents at U.S. Embassies as international attachés to coordinate investigations of wildlife trafficking and support law enforcement capacity building. The first attaché began work in Thailand last year. Others will be located in Tanzania, Peru, Botswana, and China. We are continuing to work on administrative actions called for by the National Strategy to eliminate most commercial trade in elephant ivory in the United States with certain narrow exceptions, making it harder for criminals to sell poached and trafficked ivory.

We are also providing technical assistance and grants to build in-country capacity. A substantial portion of the funding awarded through the multinational species conservation funds is invested in projects aimed at combating wildlife crime through improved law enforcement, anti-poaching patrols, demand reduction, and economic alternatives.

While we have made great strides recently to address wildlife trafficking, there is still much work to be done. The President requested $75.4 million, an increase of $8 million, for the Service's Office of Law Enforcement in Fiscal Year 2016 to combat expanding wildlife trafficking.

Wildlife crime still offers low risk and high rewards compared to drug and weapons trafficking. We need to change that calculus by stiffening penalties for wildlife crime.

Thank you for the opportunity to present testimony today. I appreciate the subcommittee's support of our efforts, and I would be pleased to answer any questions you may have.

[The prepared statement of Mr. Dreher follows:]

**TESTIMONY OF ROBERT DREHER, ASSOCIATE DIRECTOR,
U.S. FISH AND WILDLIFE SERVICE, DEPARTMENT OF THE INTERIOR,
BEFORE THE U.S. HOUSE OF REPRESENTATIVES, COMMITTEE ON FOREIGN
AFFAIRS, SUBCOMMITTEE ON TERRORISM, NONPROLIFERATION, AND TRADE
ON POACHING AND TERRORISM: A NATIONAL SECURITY CHALLENGE**

April 22, 2015

Introduction

Good afternoon Chairman Poe, Ranking Member Keating, and Members of the Subcommittee. I am Robert Dreher, Associate Director of the U.S. Fish and Wildlife Service (Service), within the Department of the Interior (Department). I appreciate the opportunity to testify before you today to discuss the escalating international wildlife trafficking crisis.

Last year, Director Ashe testified before the House Committee on Foreign Affairs and described the leadership and resources the Service has provided over the past decade that have been key to conserving imperiled wildlife and addressing illicit wildlife trade. Today, I will address how the wildlife trafficking crisis has evolved over time to one that involves highly organized criminal networks. To illustrate that, I will highlight some of our work in disrupting large-scale wildlife trafficking and the connections we have seen through our law enforcement investigations between wildlife trafficking and organized crime.

With the growing wildlife trafficking crisis, we are increasing our efforts in both our Office of Law Enforcement and International Affairs programs, and I will describe some of our recent successes within the Service and working in partnership with others in the U.S. Government. Today, I will also underscore the resources and authorities that are needed to keep up with this rapidly evolving and increasingly lucrative illicit wildlife trade.

The Wildlife Trafficking Crisis

Wildlife trafficking once was predominantly a crime of opportunity committed by individuals or small groups. Today, it is the purview of international criminal cartels that are well structured, highly organized, and capable of illegally moving large commercial volumes of wildlife and wildlife products. What was once a local or regional problem has become a global crisis, as increasingly sophisticated, violent, and ruthless criminal organizations have branched into wildlife trafficking. Organized criminal enterprises are a growing threat to wildlife, the world's economy, and global security.

Thousands of wildlife species are threatened by illegal and unsustainable wildlife trade. We have seen a resurgence of elephant poaching in Africa, which is threatening this iconic species. Africa's elephants are being slaughtered for ivory at rates not seen in decades. Populations of both savanna and forest elephants have dropped precipitously, and poaching occurs across all regions of Africa. In addition, over the past five years, the poaching of rhinos for their horns has surged upward. Tragically, the current poaching epidemic threatens to reverse fifty years of recovery for African rhinos.

Improved economic conditions in markets such as China and other parts of East and Southeast Asia are fueling an increased demand for elephant ivory, rhino horn, and other wildlife products. More Asian consumers have the financial resources to purchase these wildlife products, which are a status symbol for new economic elites. Increasingly, ivory, rhino horn and other high-value wildlife products are being acquired as investments, with speculators hoping that prices continue to rise; buyers are quite literally banking on extinction. Although the primary markets are in Asia, the United States continues to play a significant role as a major consumer and transit country for illegally traded wildlife, and we must be a part of the solution.

Wildlife Trafficking and Organized Crime

Through our law enforcement investigations, we have seen direct links between wildlife trafficking and organized crime. Our investigations have documented that individuals involved in non-wildlife crimes have branched out into wildlife crime. We see mounting evidence that wildlife crime is evolving from a crime of opportunity to one of organized crime.

Rhino Horn and Elephant Ivory Trafficking and Organized Crime

Operation Crash is an ongoing nationwide criminal investigation led by the Service that is addressing all aspects of U.S. involvement in the black market rhino horn trade, as well as the illegal trade in elephant ivory. To date, there have been 33 individuals and businesses charged and 22 convictions, with prison terms as high as 70 months. Since the launch of Operation Crash, investigators have documented the illegal sale and smuggling of hundreds of illegal rhino horns in the United States, conservatively estimated to be worth in excess of $50 million dollars on the street.

I would like to highlight three examples from Operation Crash that demonstrate the connection between wildlife trafficking and organized crime. First, in March 2014, two men from California were arrested and each was charged on a complaint in the United States District Court for the District of Nevada with one count of conspiracy to violate the Lacey Act and the Endangered Species Act (ESA), and one count of violating the Lacey Act. The subjects were charged related to the interstate trafficking in black rhino horns. One of the subjects is a felon previously linked to Colombia's infamous Medellín cocaine cartel.

A second example involved the owner of an antiques business in China, who was sentenced in May 2014 in the United States District Court for the District of New Jersey to serve 70 months in prison for heading a wildlife smuggling ring in which 30 rhino horns and numerous objects made from rhino horn and elephant ivory worth more than $4.5 million were smuggled from the United States to China. The sentence—one of the longest ever imposed for a wildlife smuggling case in the United States—was the result of 11 counts, including Lacey Act violation, conspiracy, smuggling, and making false wildlife documents. This business owner was arrested by Service special agents in January 2013 while in Miami to attend an antiques show. His "business" in that city included buying two endangered rhino horns for $59,000 from an undercover officer in a Miami Beach hotel room. In pleading guilty, he admitted he was the "boss" of three U.S. antiques dealers, including two other businessmen also convicted of related rhino horn and elephant ivory smuggling schemes.

A third example is the involvement of Irish organized crime in rhino horn trafficking. In April 2013, four stuffed rhino heads were stolen from the National Museum of Ireland's natural history section in Dublin, Ireland. This theft was attributed to an Irish organized clan, the Rathkeale Rovers, believed to be one of the world's wealthiest organized crime groups. The first signs of an Irish connection in the world of rhino horn trafficking was in January 2010, when customs officers at Ireland's Shannon Airport confiscated eight rhino horns from the baggage of two Irish passengers on a flight from Faro, Portugal. The passengers were brothers who said they were traveling antique dealers who spent most of their time living in French and German RV parks. In January 2014, as the result of a Service investigation, an Irish national known to be a member of a crime organization operating out of Ireland, was sentenced to serve 14 months in prison in New York after pleading guilty to conspiracy to violate the Lacey Act in connection with rhino horn trafficking. He was also ordered to pay a $10,000 fine and forfeit $50,000 in illegal proceeds. He had been arrested in September 2013 at Liberty International Airport in Newark, New Jersey, as he was boarding a flight to London. He admitted that he and others traveled throughout the United States buying and selling rhino horn.

Though not traditional organized crime as described by the Department of Justice, the following case involves a global conspiracy with a number of criminal participants trafficking and commercializing illegal elephant ivory. A Philadelphia businessman was sentenced in U.S. District Court in Brooklyn, New York, to 30 months imprisonment, ordered to pay a $7,500 fine, and had to forfeit $150,000 along with the approximate one ton of elephant ivory that was seized by agents from his Philadelphia store. On several occasions, he paid accomplices to acquire ivory directly from Africa and smuggle it into the United States through John F. Kennedy International Airport, which he then sold at his store. He had acquired more than 400 pieces of carved elephant ivory valued at approximately $800,000. Prior to the seizure of his ivory stockpile, he was attempting to sell his business, including the ivory collection, for $20 million. His sentence capped an 8-year investigation that yielded nine convictions for smuggling and Lacey Act offenses relating to the illegal importation and sale of elephant ivory.

Criminal Organizations - Smuggling Totoaba Bladders

Despite the Government of Mexico's increased security concerns and commitments to increase border security and dismantle illicit transnational organized crime rings operating within Mexico, criminal networks continue to emerge as major players in a number of smuggling activities to include trafficking endangered animal species, including local species such as bighorn sheep (borrego cimarrón) and the swim bladders of the endangered totoaba fish, which are smuggled back to China, where the totoaba's large swim bladder is a delicacy used in soup. The swim bladders—which fetch anywhere from $7,000 to $14,000 apiece on the black market—are taken from the Sea of Cortez and often smuggled into the United States before being smuggled to Asia. With China's growing economy, there is high demand for "exotic" cuisine, and many of the endangered animals end up as ingredients on the plates of China's upper class.

Though Chinese networks may be the most numerous and powerful, Mexican police officials report that Cambodian, Lao, and Thai groups also smuggle goods, including weapons, across the border. Those groups are particularly active in Playas de Tijuana, Popotla, and Playas de Rosarito. Mexican police officials maintain that one clique of Thai criminals launder money at Asian restaurants in Mexicali.

In 2014, a man confessed to local authorities that he killed Samuel Gallardo Castro, the leader of a Mexican organized crime group, because Gallardo Castro owed him $1 million for a shipment of totoaba swim bladders. The previous year, Mexican authorities dismantled a smuggling ring trafficking totoaba in the Sea of Cortez, seizing totoaba parts worth between $35,000 and $60,000 and arresting four people. The Service disrupted a large-scale trafficking scheme involving totoaba swim bladders. Seven individuals were indicted on Federal charges in San Diego in connection with these smuggling operations. A lead player in this trafficking, who coordinated cross-border smuggling from Mexico with plans to market the totoaba swim bladders in Asia, pled guilty to Federal charges and was sentenced to a term of imprisonment and period of probation. He was ordered to forfeit his residence (where he prepared, dried and stored the smuggled fish parts) but subsequent negotiations changed this penalty to forfeiting 75 percent of its value ($138,750) in cash. He must also pay $500,000 in restitution to support conservation programs in Mexico and forfeit 241 totoaba swim bladders.

Many Chinese gangs operating in Mexico smuggle these illicit goods north to California. Business owners confirm that it is easy to get merchandise across the border without export fees, paperwork, or even an inspection, simply by bribing border officials, who reportedly wave through Chinese textiles and appliances every day.

Recent Successes

Today's vast, globally integrated markets move at lightning speed. In order to keep up, we have to be better, faster and smarter than the criminals. This requires a multidisciplinary approach to the problem, involving law enforcement and national security, wildlife biology and conservation, finance and trade, outreach and education, and international relations and diplomacy. With the growing wildlife trafficking crisis, we are increasing our efforts, particularly in our Office of Law Enforcement and International Affairs programs, and we are working in partnership with others in the U.S. Government.

Focus across the U.S. Government on Wildlife Trafficking

The Administration recognized that if illicit wildlife trade continues on its current trajectory, some of the world's most treasured animals could be threatened with extinction. In response to this crisis, on July 1, 2013, President Obama issued Executive Order 13648 to enhance coordination of U.S. Government efforts to combat wildlife trafficking and assist foreign governments with capacity building.

The Executive Order established a Presidential Task Force on Wildlife Trafficking charged with developing and implementing a National Strategy for Combating Wildlife Trafficking. We are already improving coordination and leveraging resources across the U.S. Government. President

Obama signed the National Strategy for Combating Wildlife Trafficking on February 11, 2014. The Strategy establishes guiding principles and strategic priorities for U.S. efforts to stem illegal trade in wildlife, positioning the United States to exercise leadership in addressing this serious and urgent conservation and global security threat. It calls for strengthening the enforcement of laws and international agreements that protect wildlife while reducing demand for illegal wildlife and wildlife products. It affirms our Nation's resolve to work in partnership with governments, local communities, nongovernmental organizations, the private sector, and others to strengthen commitment to combating wildlife trafficking.

Earlier this year, the White House released the implementation plan for the National Strategy for Combating Wildlife Trafficking. The implementation plan builds on the strategy and reaffirms our Nation's commitment to work in partnership with governments, local communities, nongovernmental organizations, and the private sector to address wildlife trafficking. The plan lays out next steps, identifies lead and participating agencies for each objective, and defines how we will measure progress in implementing the strategy.

Trans-Pacific Partnership

An important component of our fight against wildlife trafficking is the inclusion of anti-trafficking efforts in international trade agreements. In the Trans-Pacific Partnership (TPP) negotiations with eleven other countries in the Asia-Pacific, the Administration is on track to secure historic commitments to combat wildlife trafficking and provide strengthened protections for wildlife. The TPP would commit countries to implementing, strengthening, and enforcing laws that protect threatened and endangered species like rhinos and pangolins, and to matching new protections with cooperative tools that will spur and support regional action. This is critical as the TPP countries include some of the world's most biologically diverse and ecologically significant regions. One of the key features of the TPP would be that all commitments would be fully enforceable and subject to trade sanctions – a powerful tool to catalyze strong and sustained action to address this environmental crisis.

U.S. Ivory Crush

We took an enormous step forward in 2013 when we joined Kenya, the Philippines, and Gabon in crushing our stock of illegal ivory. In November of that year, the United States destroyed its 6-ton stock of confiscated elephant ivory. This sent a clear message that we will not tolerate wildlife crime that threatens to wipe out the African elephant, rhinoceroses, and a host of other species around the globe. Several other governments—including the People's Republic of China, Chad, France, Belgium, Hong Kong, Kenya, and Ethiopia—have since followed suit. We now are in a much better position to work with the international community to push for a reduction of illegal ivory stockpiles worldwide, and crack down on poaching and illegal wildlife trade.

Reauthorization of the Save Vanishing Species Stamp

In 2014, Congress and the President also took a significant step by enacting the Multinational Species Conservation Funds Semipostal Stamp Reauthorization Act, meaning once again, Americans can purchase the Save Vanishing Species Stamp at post offices and online. The stamp functions as a regular postal stamp that sells at a small premium. The additional money goes to the Service's Multinational Species Conservation Funds, directly funding conservation of elephants, rhinos, tigers, great apes, and marine turtles. Since the stamp's inception in 2011, more than 26 million stamps have been purchased by the American public, generating more than $2.6 million for conservation.

Stationing Service Law Enforcement Overseas

Wildlife trafficking is increasingly a transnational crime involving illicit activities in two or more countries and often two or more global regions. Cooperation between nations is essential to combat this crime. With assistance from the State Department, we have created the first program for stationing Service law enforcement special agents at U.S. embassies as international attachés to coordinate investigations of wildlife trafficking and support wildlife enforcement capacity building. The first attaché began work in March 2014 in Bangkok, Thailand. We have selected three more attachés and plan on having them in the following three locations: Dar es Salaam, Tanzania; Lima, Peru; and Gaborone, Botswana. We are continuing to work on placing a fifth attaché in China.

Restricting Commercial Trade in Elephant Ivory and other Protected Species

We have made great strides to significantly restrict commercial trade in elephant ivory within the United States and across our borders—including a ban on all commercial ivory imports—making it harder for criminals to disguise the source of poached and trafficked ivory.

The Service issued Director's Order 210, which re-affirmed enforcement of the African Elephant Conservation Act moratorium and addressed how the Service would enforce the ESA antiques provision. We also improved our ability to protect elephants, rhinos, tigers, and other CITES-listed wildlife by publishing a final rule in June 2014 revising our CITES regulations, including "use after import" provisions that limit sale of CITES-listed wildlife within the United States. The result of this rule is that items, such as elephant ivory, imported for noncommercial purposes may not subsequently be sold within the United States. We will also publish a proposed rule, available for public comment, to revise the ESA special rule for the African elephant, which will include proposed limitations on the interstate sale of African elephant ivory.

Technical Assistance and Grants to Build In-Country Capacity

Through the Multinational Species Conservation Funds, the Service funds projects benefiting elephants, rhinos, tigers, great apes, and marine turtles. A substantial portion of the funding awarded through these grants is invested in projects aimed at combating wildlife crime through improved law enforcement, anti-poaching patrols, demand reduction, and economic alternatives.

Through the Wildlife Without Borders – Africa Program, a technical and financial partnership with USAID, the Service has supported the development of innovative methods to conserve wildlife and fight wildlife crime in Central Africa, including strengthening investigative and prosecutorial capacity. A number of projects are geared toward building in-country capacity and providing technical assistance to reduce the poaching of African elephants.

Future Challenges and Needs

While we have made great strides recently to address wildlife trafficking, there is still much work to be done.

Increasing Capacity to Address Wildlife Trafficking

The President requested $75.4 million, an increase of $8 million, for the Service's Office of Law Enforcement in FY 2016 to combat expanding illegal wildlife trafficking and support conservation efforts on-the-ground in Africa and across the globe. This additional funding would also expand the Service's wildlife forensics capability to provide the evidence needed for investigating and prosecuting criminal activity.

Strengthening Legal Authorities

We need to do more to target and disrupt the sophisticated, violent and ruthless criminal organizations increasingly branching out into wildlife crime. For these criminals, wildlife crime still offers low risk and high rewards compared to drug and weapons trafficking. We need to change that calculus, treating transnational wildlife crime as the pernicious threat to global stability, security, and the environment that it is. This includes stiffening penalties for wildlife crimes in consumer nations as well as range countries.

The Administration's National Strategy for Combating Wildlife Trafficking called on Congress to consider legislation to recognize wildlife trafficking crimes as predicate offenses for money laundering and to ensure that funds generated through prosecutions are directed back to conservation efforts or to combating wildlife trafficking. These actions would be invaluable to the Service's law enforcement efforts because they would help place wildlife trafficking on an equal footing with other serious crimes. We commend Senator Dianne Feinstein and Senator Lindsey Graham for introducing S. 27, the Wildlife Trafficking Enforcement Act, which would take steps toward these important goals. Changing the law in this area is key to ending the days of wildlife trafficking being a low-risk, high-profit crime.

Conclusion

Thank you for the opportunity to present testimony today. I appreciate the Subcommittee's support of our efforts to combat wildlife trafficking. I look forward to working with you to ensure a secure future for imperiled species across the globe. I would be pleased to answer any questions that you may have.

Mr. POE. Thank you, Mr. Dreher.

Mr. Cruden, your opening statement.

STATEMENT OF THE HONORABLE JOHN CRUDEN, ASSISTANT ATTORNEY GENERAL, ENVIRONMENT AND NATURAL RESOURCES DIVISION, U.S. DEPARTMENT OF JUSTICE

Mr. CRUDEN. Chairman Poe and Ranking Member Keating, thank you again for the opportunity to discuss the work of the Environment and Natural Resources Division of the Department of Justice with respect to combating illegal wildlife trafficking. You have my prepared testimony, which I request that you add to the record.

But I want to highlight three things out of that testimony: I want to talk to you a little bit about the key role of our environmental prosecutors, our environmental criminal section—we are prosecuting wildlife criminals—and then, finally, a little bit following up on one of your questions, and that is our work in training and building capacity abroad.

The Environment Division through the Environmental Crime Section is a recognized leader in the fight against wildlife trafficking. The recent Executive order on combating wildlife trafficking brought increased attention to the severity of really a global crisis that we are facing now. Wildlife trafficking, which includes poaching protected species and trafficking in their parts, has become a highly profitable crime with profits in the billions of dollars. Illegal activity at this scale has devastating impacts. It threatens security. It hinders sustainable economic development. It undermines the rule of law. And the illicit trade in wildlife is decimating many species worldwide, and some of those species, including such majestic animals as rhinoceroses, elephants, great apes, sharks and tigers, face extinction in our time or maybe our children's time.

The National Strategy for Combating Wildlife Trafficking identifies three priorities: Strengthening enforcement, reducing demand, and building global cooperation. Just last month I had the honor of being, along with Bob Dreher, at the U.S. delegation to the Kasane Conference in Botswana on Illegal Wildlife Trade, where the ranking leaders from more than 30 nations came together to discuss both the problem and the need to work together to address the crisis. I spoke on behalf of the United States about our efforts to combat wildlife trafficking, but I had the opportunity then to discuss with many African leaders the challenges that they are facing. My testimony today is influenced by those comments.

You know this: At DOJ, we prosecute. The Environment Division along with U.S. attorneys across the country in partnership with Fish and Wildlife Service is responsible for prosecuting wildlife trafficking crimes, including related crimes, things like smuggling, money laundering, conspiracies. This is serious crime, and we treat it seriously. And we seek significant periods of incarceration, fines, restitution, community service to help mitigate the harm caused by the offense; forfeiture of wildlife and instrumentalities used to commit the offense; and, where possible, disgorgement of the proceeds of the illegal conduct.

You just heard from Bob Dreher about Operation Crash, which was a multi-agency effort. It resulted in more than 20 successful prosecutions, and you saw some of the defendants in the slide that was presented. I put in my prepared testimony a whole series of descriptions of other wildlife criminal enforcement that we have done in the relatively recent past. I just wanted to give you an idea of what is happening on the ground right now. I don't think there will be any question of this, that we are recognized throughout the world as the leader in wildlife prosecutions.

In addition to our own direct prosecution, however, we are also doing capacity building right now. Through the assistance of the State Department, we are developing a new program in Africa that will focus on wildlife trafficking. We are planning two regional programs: The first will go in Southeast Africa; the second in central West Africa. And we are focusing on prosecutors and judges.

Just last week I met with some of the leaders of a new task force from Togo. We told them about what we were doing. They told us that is exactly what they needed. We are also participating extensively in trading in wildlife enforcement networks. These are the networks of prosecutors who come together to try to share experience and gain from others.

We are proud of what we have done, but there is so much more to do. We know that we need to be focusing our efforts on bringing down high-level traffickers, closing their networks, and disrupting the illegal funding flows. We are seeking to take the profit out of wildlife trafficking by using all the tools that are available to us. We look forward to working with you and Congress to strengthen our legal framework, and we would welcome the opportunity to talk about such steps as recognizing wildlife trafficking as a predicate crime for money laundering and RICO offenses. Another important step could be legislation authorizing forfeiture of all proceeds gained by illegal wildlife trafficking.

In closing, the Department, working with other agencies, particularly those two that are sharing right now—Department of State and Fish and Wildlife Service—we look forward to vigorously prosecuting those who poach and traffic illegally in wildlife across the world.

Thank you. Happy to answer any questions you might have.

[The prepared statement of Mr. Cruden follows:]

Department of Justice

STATEMENT
OF

JOHN C. CRUDEN
ASSISTANT ATTORNEY GENERAL
ENVIRONMENT AND NATURAL RESOURCES DIVISION

FOR THE

COMMITTEE ON FOREIGN AFFAIRS
SUBCOMMITTEE ON TERRORISM,
NONPROLIFERATION, AND TRADE
U.S. HOUSE OF REPRESENTATIVES

HEARING ENTITLED

"POACHING AND TERRORISM: A NATIONAL SECURITY CHALLENGE"

ON

APRIL 22, 2015

STATEMENT OF
JOHN C. CRUDEN
ASSISTANT ATTORNEY GENERAL
ENVIRONMENT AND NATURAL RESOURCES DIVISION
DEPARTMENT OF JUSTICE

BEFORE THE
COMMITTEE ON FOREIGN AFFAIRS
SUBCOMMITTEE ON TERRORISM,
NONPROLIFERATION, AND TRADE
U.S. HOUSE OF REPRESENTATIVES

"POACHING AND TERRORISM: A NATIONAL SECURITY CHALLENGE"

April 22, 2015

I.   INTRODUCTION

Chairman Poe, and Members of the Committee on Foreign Affairs Subcommittee on Terrorism, Nonproliferation, and Trade, thank you for the opportunity to submit to you this testimony discussing the work of the Environment and Natural Resources Division of the U.S. Department of Justice ("ENRD" or the "Environment Division") with respect to the Administration's efforts to combat wildlife trafficking.

II.   OVERVIEW OF THE ENVIRONMENT AND NATURAL RESOURCES DIVISION

The Environment and Natural Resources Division is a core litigating component of the U.S. Department of Justice (the "Department"). Founded more than a century ago, ENRD has built a distinguished record of legal excellence. The Division is organized into nine litigating sections (Appellate; Environmental Crimes; Environmental Defense; Environmental Enforcement; Indian Resources; Land Acquisition; Law and Policy; Natural Resources; and Wildlife and Marine Resources), and an Executive Office that provides administrative support. ENRD has a staff of about 600, more than 400 of whom are attorneys.

The Division functions as the Nation's environmental lawyer, representing virtually every federal agency in courts across the United States and its territories and possessions in civil and criminal cases that arise under an array of federal statutes. Our work furthers the Department's strategic goals to prevent crime and enforce federal laws, defend the interests of the United States, promote national security, and ensure the fair administration of justice at the federal, state, local, and tribal levels.

III. ENRD'S WORK WITH RESPECT TO WILDLIFE TRAFFICKING

For the purposes of this hearing, this testimony highlights the work the Division is doing to address the increasing global crisis posed by international wildlife trafficking. This work includes prosecuting wildlife traffickers; conducting capacity-building and training on these and related issues; and implementing the National Strategy for Combating Wildlife Trafficking, as well as the Action Plan for Implementing the Recommendations of the Presidential Task Force on Combating Illegal, Unreported, and Unregulated (IUU) Fishing and Seafood Fraud.

The Department of Justice, principally through the work of the Environment Division, has long been a leader in the fight against wildlife trafficking. The President's Executive Order on Combating Wildlife Trafficking, issued on July 1, 2013, and the Presidential Memorandum on Establishing a Comprehensive Framework to Combat IUU Fishing and Seafood Fraud, issued on June 17, 2014, brought increased attention to the severity of the crisis we are facing. Wildlife trafficking—which includes poaching of protected species and trafficking in their parts—has become one of the most profitable types of transnational organized crime. Illegal trade at this scale has devastating impacts: it threatens security, hinders sustainable economic development, and undermines the rule of law. The illicit trade in wildlife is decimating many species worldwide, and some species—including such majestic animals as rhinoceroses, elephants, great apes, totoaba, sea turtles, and tigers—face extinction in our lifetimes or our children's lifetimes.

The Executive Order recognized the urgent need for concerted action and called for a new approach, establishing a Presidential Task Force on Wildlife Trafficking to lead a coordinated, government-wide effort to stop poaching and other wildlife trafficking. The Task Force, which the Department of Justice co-chairs along with the Departments of State and the Interior, includes the Departments of Treasury, Defense, Agriculture, Commerce, Transportation, and Homeland Security, as well as the United States Agency for International Development and seven other federal departments and agencies. The Task Force receives input from an Advisory Council that includes experts who have a wide range of experience and skills and who represent many of the different communities that must be engaged as partners to tackle this problem.

In February 2014, the White House issued the National Strategy for Combating Wildlife Trafficking, based on the work of the Task Force. The Strategy reflects a "whole of government" approach and calls for increased federal coordination to address three key priorities: (1) strengthening domestic and international law enforcement to curb the illegal flow of wildlife; (2) reducing the demand for illegally traded wildlife; and (3) building global cooperation and public/private partnerships to support the fight against wildlife trafficking.

The Task Force agencies have been working in coordination to implement the Strategy since its issuance, and in February of this year, the Task Force released an Implementation Plan that builds upon the Strategy. The Implementation Plan provides a robust, focused reaffirmation of the Nation's commitment to stopping wildlife trafficking, and sets out specific steps to achieve each strategic priority.

The Presidential Memorandum on IUU Fishing recognized a similar and related need for action focused specifically on the effort to combat trafficking in illegally harvested fish, among other things. That Memorandum established a Presidential Task Force on Combating IUU

Fishing and Seafood Fraud, co-chaired by the Departments of Commerce and State, of which the Department of Justice is a member. The IUU Task Force published a set of recommendations for actions to combat IUU fishing and seafood fraud in December 2014, and followed those recommendations up just last month with its Action Plan for Implementing the Recommendations of the Presidential Task Force on IUU Fishing and Seafood Fraud. That Action Plan sets out specific steps to implement each recommendation.

We recognize that this is a global problem that needs a global response, and success will require a significant and sustained commitment over the long term. International wildlife traffickers respect no international borders, so it is essential that the United States coordinate with foreign governments to stop this cross-border crime. The Administration is committed to working closely with foreign governments, non-governmental organizations, the private sector, community leaders, and civil society to take the steps needed to develop and implement effective solutions that address all aspects of wildlife trafficking, from poaching and transit through consumer use. Range states, transit states, and consumer states must all work together to counter this transnational threat.

Combating wildlife trafficking is a top priority for the Department. Just last month, I led the U.S. delegation to the Kasane Conference on the Illegal Wildlife Trade, where representatives from more than 30 nations gathered to follow up on the commitments made at last year's London Conference, at which Associate Attorney General Tony West led the United States delegation. The joint participation of the United States Departments of Justice, State, and the Interior at these Conferences demonstrates the "whole of government" approach taken in the National Strategy, which we are pleased to see other nations beginning to adopt as well. It was a true honor to speak on behalf of the United States about our ongoing efforts to combat wildlife trafficking through the National Strategy and the newly released Implementation Plan. While in Botswana, we also participated in the second African Elephant Summit, which focused on international efforts to implement 14 "urgent measures" adopted at the first African Elephant Summit in 2013 to stop the illegal slaughter of elephants for their ivory.

The Department of Justice looks forward to continuing to work closely with the other members of the Task Force on implementation of all aspects of the Strategy, though our primary efforts naturally focus on enforcement. The Strategy and the Action Plan on IUU Fishing recognize that strong enforcement, both at home and abroad, is critical to stopping those who kill and traffic in protected animals, whether on land or in the oceans. The work we do to improve domestic and global enforcement includes not only our own case work but also our substantial efforts to improve enforcement through international capacity-building and training. The Department of Justice has for many years aggressively pursued and prosecuted those engaged in the illegal wildlife trade. We have also worked vigorously to train and support partner countries in their efforts to stanch this terrible crime.

A.   Wildlife Trafficking Prosecutions

The Division has a section devoted to the prosecution of environmental crimes, including wildlife crime. The Environmental Crimes Section has 38 dedicated criminal prosecutors who often work together with U.S. Attorneys' Offices around the country and our federal agency partners (such as the U.S. Fish and Wildlife Service and the National Oceanic and Atmospheric Administration) in the area of wildlife trafficking. We have had significant successes over the years prosecuting those who smuggle and traffic in elephant ivory, endangered rhinoceros horns, South African leopard, Asian and African tortoises and reptiles, paddlefish eggs, and many other forms of protected wildlife. Some cases that exemplify these critical enforcement efforts are discussed below.

The two primary federal anti-wildlife trafficking statutes that the Department enforces are the Lacey Act and the Endangered Species Act. The Lacey Act reaches two broad categories of wildlife offenses: illegal trafficking in wildlife and false labeling. The Endangered Species Act establishes a U.S. program for the conservation of endangered and threatened species. The Endangered Species Act makes it illegal to traffic in listed endangered or threatened species without a permit and also implements our international treaty obligations under the Convention on International Trade in Endangered Species of Wild Fauna and Flora (CITES)—a treaty establishing limits on trade in certain species of wildlife. In addition, the Marine Mammal Protection Act prohibits the illegal take and importation of marine mammals and marine mammal products, providing additional protections against trafficking in these species.

The types of cases we prosecute for illegal trafficking are varied. While many involve individuals trafficking in illegal wildlife and wildlife parts, we are also seeing the involvement of criminal organizations, including transnational criminal organizations that may threaten the security interests of the U.S. and its allies. We routinely seek punishment that includes sentences for significant periods of incarceration, fines, and restitution or community service to help mitigate harm caused by the offense; forfeiture of the wildlife and instrumentalities used to commit the offense; and, where wildlife traffickers also violate laws against smuggling or other related crimes, disgorgement of the proceeds of the illegal conduct.

A prominent example of the Division's robust prosecution of illegal wildlife trafficking is "Operation Crash," an ongoing multi-agency effort to detect, deter, and prosecute those engaged in the illegal killing of rhinoceros and the illegal trafficking of endangered rhinoceros horns. This initiative has resulted in 20 successful prosecutions thus far, and we are continuing to unravel the sophisticated international criminal networks involved in these crimes. Defendants in these cases have been sentenced to significant terms of imprisonment and the forfeiture of millions of dollars in cash, gold bars, rhino horn, and luxury vehicles and jewelry.

In one case, *United States v. Zhifei Li* (D.N.J.), the defendant, owner of Overseas Treasure Finding in Shandong, China, was sentenced last year to serve 70 months' incarceration. He also will forfeit $3.5 million in proceeds from his criminal activity as well as several Asian artifacts. Li was in the business of selling raw rhino horns to factories where they would be carved into fake antiques and then resold. Horns that Li acquired were smuggled across international borders. The horns were hidden by a variety of means, including wrapping them in duct tape, hiding them in porcelain vases that were falsely described on customs and shipping documents, and labeling them as porcelain vases or handicrafts. The pieces left over from the carving process were sold for alleged "medicinal" purposes. Rhino carvings valued at as much as $242,500 were sold to Li's customers in China. Shortly after arriving in the United States in January 2013, Li was arrested in Florida on federal charges brought under seal in New Jersey.

Prior to his arrest, he had purchased two endangered black rhinoceros horns from an undercover U.S. Fish and Wildlife Service agent in a Miami Beach hotel room for $59,000 while attending an antique show. Li admitted to organizing an illegal wildlife smuggling conspiracy in which 30 raw rhinoceros horns and numerous objects made from rhino horn and elephant ivory (worth more than $4.5 million) were smuggled from the United States to China. Li admitted that he was the "boss" of three antique dealers in the United States whom he paid to help obtain wildlife items and smuggle to him through Hong Kong. One of those individuals was Qiang Wang, a/k/a "Jeffrey Wang," who was sentenced to serve 37 months' incarceration for smuggling Asian artifacts, including "libation cups," made from rhinoceros horn and ivory (*United States v. Qiang Wang* (S.D.N.Y.)). Another was Ning Qiu, an art appraiser who admitted traveling throughout the United States to purchase raw and carved rhinoceros horns and elephant ivory and smuggling it to Hong Kong. More information about the Li case is available at http://www.justice.gov/usao/nj/Press/files/Li,%20Zhifei%20Sentencing%20PR.html; information about the Wang case is at http://www.justice.gov/opa/pr/2013/December/13-enrd-1284.html and the Qiu case is at http://www.justice.gov/opa/pr/texas-man-pleads-guilty-rhino-and-ivory-smuggling-conspiracy.

Another recent "Operation Crash" success is *United States v. Xiao Ju Guan a/k/a "Tony Guan"* (S.D.N.Y.). The defendant was sentenced just last month to 30 months in prison for smuggling rhinoceros horns, elephant ivory, and coral from the United States to Canada. The defendant is a Canadian citizen and the owner of Bao Antiques, a company based in Canada and Hong Kong. Guan and co-conspirators smuggled more than $500,000 of rhino horns and sculptures made from elephant ivory and coral from various U.S. auction houses to Canada by driving them across the border or by having packages mailed directly to Canada with false paperwork and without the required declaration or permits. A rhino horn purchased in Florida, for example, was described on Customs paperwork as a "Wooden Horn" worth $200. Guan was arrested in New York after attempting to purchase two endangered black rhinoceros horns for $45,000 from undercover U.S. FWS agents. At the same time he was arrested, Canadian authorities executed a search warrant at his antique business in Canada, seizing multiple wildlife objects that had been smuggled out of the United States. During the search of Guan's business, Canadian enforcement discovered illegal narcotics, including approximately 50,000 ecstasy pills. More information about this case is available at http://www.justice.gov/opa/pr/canadian-antiques-dealer-sentenced-30-months-prison-smuggling-rhinoceros-horns-elephant-ivory.

In another case, *United States v. Michael Slattery, Jr.*, (E.D.N.Y.), Slattery was sentenced to serve 14 months' incarceration, followed by three years' supervised release. Slattery also will pay a $10,000 fine and forfeit $50,000 of proceeds from his illegal trade in rhinoceros horns. In 2010, Slattery, an Irish national, traveled from England to Texas to acquire black rhinoceros horns. Mr. Slattery admitted to illegal trafficking throughout the United States and is alleged to belong to an organized criminal group engaged in rhino horn trafficking. This organized criminal element speaks to the scope, scale, and lawlessness of this problem. More information about this case is available at: http://www.justice.gov/opa/pr/2013/November/13-enrd-1181.html.

"Operation Crash" has also targeted criminals for their role in illegal rhino hunts. In *United States v. Dawie Groenewald et al.* (M.D. Ala.), an indictment was unsealed on October

23, 2014, charging South African nationals, brothers Dawie and Janneman Groenewald, and their company, a large game hunting business, with conspiracy to violate the Lacey Act, and to commit mail fraud and money laundering. Defendants allegedly sold illegal rhino hunts to American hunters at U.S. hunting shows. The hunters were each told a similar story about how the particular rhino that they would hunt was a problem animal that needed to be killed and so no export permit was available. Instead, the cost of the hunt was considerably less ($10,000 or less) than one where a hunter could bring back a trophy. The defendants sold the horns from the rhinos killed in the scheme to contacts who smuggled the horns to Asia. The hunts themselves were unlawful because they were conducted in violation of South African law and without required hunting permits. This scheme was hidden from the American hunters, typically through a series of misleading and/or false representations that led the American hunters to assume or believe that the hunts were legal. During the period of the conspiracy, Janneman lived in Alabama. Dawie Groenewald was previously convicted in 2010 in federal court in Alabama for his role in smuggling a leopard skin into the United States. In addition, in September 2010, he, his wife, and ten others were arrested and charged in South Africa on 1,872 counts of racketeering, including illegal trade in rhinoceros horns. http://www.justice.gov/opa/pr/owners-safari-company-indicted-illegal-rhino-hunts

"Operation Crash" cases, like the *Li* and *Guan* cases above, may also include charges related to the illegal smuggling and sale of elephant ivory. The Division has seen success in other elephant ivory cases. In *United States v. Victor Gordon*, the defendant was sentenced to 30 months' imprisonment for smuggling elephant ivory into the United States. Gordon also forfeited the approximately one ton of ivory seized from his store—one of the largest single ivory seizures in United States history—as well as an additional $150,000. In some instances, Gordon stained the ivory that he was smuggling into the country from Africa and directed the smuggler to create false receipts to disguise its origin. More information about this case is available at http://www.justice.gov/usao/nye/pr/June14/2014June4.php.

Another ivory case, *United States v. Kemo Sylla, et al.* (E.D.N.Y.), concerned the illegal importation of ivory over a two-year period through New York's JFK Airport. The ivory was disguised as African handicrafts and wooden instruments. The six defendants pleaded guilty to Lacey Act violations and received sentences ranging from one year of probation to 14 months' incarceration. A number of the defendants also were ordered to pay fines to the Lacey Act Reward Fund. More information about this case is available at: www.justice.gov/usao/nye/pr/2011/2011mar03.html.

Still other prosecutions involve the illegal import or export of endangered species. For instance, in *United States v. Nathaniel Swanson* (W.D. Wash.), three defendants were recently sentenced (following guilty pleas) to incarceration ranging from 5 months to one year, supervised release, and an order to pay $28,583 in restitution for conspiracy to smuggle various turtle and reptile species from the United States to Hong Kong, including Eastern box turtles, North American wood turtles, and ornate box turtles. One of the defendants also illegally imported several protected turtle species from Hong Kong, including black-breasted leaf turtles, Chinese striped-necked turtles, big-headed turtles, fly river turtles, and an Arakan forest turtle. The Arakan forest turtle is critically endangered, having once been presumed extinct. The illegal trafficking spanned approximately four years. More information about this case is available at http://www.justice.gov/usao/waw/press/2014/January/swanson.html.

B.   Working in the International Sphere: Training and Capacity-Building

As the Strategy recognizes, the United States has an important role to play in strengthening enforcement not only here at home but around the globe. For many years, prosecutors and other Division attorneys have worked closely with our foreign government partners to build their capacity to develop and effectively enforce their wildlife trafficking laws, better enabling them to combat local poaching and the attendant illegal wildlife trade. We conduct our international training in close collaboration with the Department of State and other federal agencies, such as the Department of the Interior, the U.S. Forest Service and the US Agency for International Development.

The Division's training efforts have focused on the legal, investigative, and prosecutorial aspects of fighting wildlife crime. We seek to help our partners craft strong laws, strengthen their investigation and evidence-gathering capabilities, and improve their judicial and prosecutorial effectiveness. Our experience has shown that such training develops more effective partners to investigate and prosecute transnational environmental crimes, increases our ability to enforce U.S. criminal statutes that have extraterritorial dimensions while also helping law enforcement officials in the U.S. and other countries meet their enforcement obligations under international environmental and free trade agreements. These training initiatives also foster positive relationships with prosecutors in other countries in a way that better enables us to share information and assist in prosecuting transnational crimes.

Capacity-building may be conducted bilaterally (in the United States or a partner nation) or in multilateral fora, and our programs may span a range of environmental crimes. Right now, we are working with the State Department to develop a new capacity building program for prosecutors and judges in Africa that will focus on wildlife trafficking. We are planning two regional programs, with an initial session focused on countries in south-east Africa and a second session in central-west Africa. The program will include an important follow-on component that will allow us to continue working with our African counterparts as they put the training into effect. Just last week, I had the opportunity, through the Department of State's International Visitor Leadership Program, to sit down with two members of Togo's recently formed interagency task force on wildlife trafficking. Togo has been very active in combating wildlife trafficking and has had some important successes in recent years, including seizures of more than four tons of illegal ivory. The Togolese delegation to the United States shared with us their goals for this program, and explained that they see regional trainings such as this as essential to the fight against wildlife trafficking.

The Division has participated extensively in training and providing support for foreign investigators, prosecutors, and judges through the various Wildlife Enforcement Networks ("WENs"). These include the Association of Southeast Asian Nations WEN ("ASEAN-WEN"), South Asia WEN, and Central American WEN, as well as the launch of WENs in Central Africa, Southern Africa, and the Horn of Africa. In multiple countries in these regions, we have conducted workshops that involved dozens of agencies from the host countries, and typically have included hundreds of participants representing government, the judiciary, industry, and civil society. The workshops are a mix of direct course instruction on legal and wildlife trafficking enforcement issues, including presentations by U.S. environmental prosecutors, and an opportunity for representatives from the different countries to exchange views on the issues they face. Thus, these sessions are both a valuable training opportunity and an opportunity to develop a law enforcement network in that region.

The Division has also been involved in numerous international training efforts focused on enhancing prosecutions brought under the Lacey Act, the United States' oldest plant and wildlife protection statute. With the amendment of the Lacey Act in 2008 to protect a broader range of plants and plant products, much of our recent capacity-building work has focused on the trade in illegally harvested and traded timber and timber products, an illegal trade conservatively estimated at a value of $10 to $15 billion worldwide. The National Strategy recognizes that wildlife trafficking is facilitated and exacerbated by the illegal harvest and trade in plants and trees, which destroys needed habitat and opens access to previously remote populations of highly endangered wildlife.

ENRD has conducted numerous training sessions abroad on investigating and prosecuting illegal logging cases in Indonesia, Brazil, Peru, Honduras, and Russia with financial support from the State Department and the Agency for International Development. The training agenda may vary somewhat from country to country, but is typically done in close collaboration with the foreign government and local prosecutors. We ordinarily include wildlife trafficking as a component of this training. ENRD is also working closely with the Department of Agriculture's Animal and Plant Health Inspection Service and Forest Service to collaborate with the European Union and Australia as all three move forward on implementing and enforcing new, complementary laws and regulations addressing the illegal timber trade. Such collaboration benefits and strengthens criminal law enforcement in both countries.

The Division conducts further international capacity-building in the area of illegal wildlife trafficking through its participation in INTERPOL (specifically the Wildlife Crime Working Group, Environmental Crime Committee, and Fisheries Crime Working Group) and the International Law Enforcement Academy (with programs for eastern European and Southeast Asian law enforcement officials).

C. Continuing to Implement the National Strategy to Combat Wildlife Trafficking

The Department is proud of its record of achievement in this area, but we all recognize that much remains to be done. Moving forward, the Implementation Plan provides an important framework for our efforts. As detailed in the Implementation Plan, the Department will focus its efforts on a wide variety of activities intended to strengthen enforcement both at home and abroad.

Department prosecutors will continue to target traffickers and their networks, consistent with the enforcement goals and priorities laid out in the National Strategy and the Implementation Plan. We will focus on bringing down high-level traffickers and on disrupting the illicit funding flows that wildlife trafficking facilitates. We will seek to make illegal wildlife trafficking much less profitable by using the tools of fines and penalties, seizure and forfeiture, and payment of restitution to those victimized by illegal trafficking. The Department will also strengthen our coordination of enforcement efforts, looking for ways to improve the way we work with our federal partner agencies (including through the improved sharing of intelligence), as well as state and tribal authorities. One recent example of our increased effort and attention to prosecuting wildlife trafficking is the Department's decision to devote two of the six issues of the U.S. Attorneys' Bulletin being published this year exclusively to wildlife crime and related issues. We have also increased our efforts to provide training for U.S. personnel stationed abroad to ensure that they are prepared to support our efforts to combat wildlife trafficking.

We look forward to continuing to work with Congress to strengthen existing laws and develop new legislation to improve the tools available to address this challenge. The law should place wildlife trafficking on an equal footing with other serious crimes, for example, by recognizing wildlife trafficking as a predicate crime for money laundering. We can also more effectively fight the scourge of wildlife trafficking if Congress passes legislation that allows for using funds generated through wildlife trafficking prosecutions to mitigate the harms caused by that trafficking, as well as to ensure adequate authority to forfeit all proceeds of wildlife trafficking.

Looking globally, the Department will continue to help source, transit, and demand countries build their capacity to take action against illegal wildlife traffickers. Given the transnational dimension of this problem, we will increase our efforts to support our foreign partners in this area. We will continue our support and training of existing Wildlife Enforcement Networks and look to support additional regional WENs, where appropriate. And more directly, recognizing that illegal wildlife trafficking is a growing area of transnational organized crime, we will support and engage in enforcement initiatives together with the enforcement authorities of other nations. These efforts will target the assets and seek to impede the financial capacity of international wildlife traffickers.

IV.   CONCLUSION

In closing, the Department remains fully committed to working with the Administration and Congress to do all that we can to stop those who poach and traffic illegally in wildlife.

Mr. POE. I recognize myself for some questions and recognize you all for the answers. It is important that we, as you have all said, understand as Americans the consequences of doing nothing. The disappearance of elephants, it is hard to imagine that that would happen in this world, but it could.

And as Mr. Cruden has said, in our lifetime and in our kids' lifetime, the only place they are going to see an elephant is in a Disney cartoon maybe because there won't be any. And rhinos are in worse shape and tigers as well.

I am going to focus my questions on terrorism, terrorist groups, poaching, where they sell these items, and the money that is involved. Do we have any idea how many terrorist organizations are involved in Africa in the poaching business?

Ambassador.

Ambassador GARBER. Thank you, Mr. Chairman. This is an illicit trade by its very nature. So, of course, it is something that it is difficult for us to have very firm knowledge about. There is no question that the shadowing adaptive financial flows that fund illicit crime and illicit activities are at play. We do have evidence that militant groups, such as the Lord's Resistance Army and Janjaweed, benefit substantially from illegal trade in wildlife. Some terrorist entities we believe are benefitting, but the details are very sketchy. By how much, it is very hard for us to know.

Mr. POE. I understand that in the Democratic Republic of the Congo, 150 park rangers have been killed since 2004, and according to the International Ranger Federation, worldwide, park rangers, two are killed every week that are protecting these parks where all these animals are. It seems to me that the Lord's Resistance Army, which you mentioned, is using Garamba National Park in the Democratic Republic of Congo as a base of operations. What can you say a little more specifically about the connections between the LRA and the ivory trade as a source of its financing?

Ambassador GARBER. I can say the Lord's Resistance Army is deriving significant revenue from poaching and illegal trade in elephants, and we have seen these activities intensify over the last 2 years.

Mr. POE. Under current law, the U.S. Government can deny a foreigner a visa if they are convicted of human trafficking, terrorist activity, violations of religious freedom. Do you think we should add wildlife trafficking to that list, Ambassador?

Ambassador GARBER. It is something that we could consider. We need—I think part of what we need to be doing is, as you said very clearly in your statement, Mr. Chairman, is that we really need to understand what is going on better and in more depth. And that is something that I think the National Wildlife Strategy and the task force has really done. We have seen the strategy and the whole-of-government approach truly elevate the attention that the intelligence community is giving this problem; we are being able to identify the gaps in what our knowledge is and where we need to focus that. And I think as that all becomes clear, we will be in a better position to really understand if that kind of a step is what makes the most sense at this time.

Mr. POE. If U.S. law enforcement suspects a foreign-owned-and-operated outfitter of violating wildlife laws in a foreign country and the foreign country refuses to arrest or prosecute the owners and operators, does the United States have any enforcement actions, such as denying or freezing assets, Mr. Cruden?

Can we do anything about that?

Mr. CRUDEN. When we are bringing our prosecutions, we are doing it fundamentally under the Lacey Act and the Endangered Species Act. Under the Lacey Act, where we actually do look violations of host country laws, but we are looking at that with a nexus to us. They are violating the laws, and they are coming to the United States. And so that is the connection that we have right now.

By the way, the Lacey Act is, in fact, a model for the rest of the world. In country after country that we are talking to, they are talking about whether or not they would emulate something like the Lacey Act, so I do not want to minimize its importance right now. But it does require that nexus to the United States before we would have the ability to prosecute.

Mr. POE. By ''nexus'' you mean what?

Mr. CRUDEN. By coming into the United States. You are importing something into or exporting something out of the United States.

Mr. POE. We deal with international drug cartels, and my understanding is they don't have to physically be on the United States land to go and prosecute them if the money chain comes into the U.S. Is that right or not?

Mr. CRUDEN. I believe that you are correct. Still the same issue, that there has to be some connection to the United States. But, by the way, under drug trafficking laws, those are a predicate offense to money laundering, an ability we really don't have under wildlife trafficking laws. So drug laws are, in fact, more powerful than some of our wildlife trafficking offenses, which is why I brought that up in my testimony, that that was something else that we would be interested in exploring with you.

Mr. POE. So, if I understand you correctly, if we could balance the enforcement with—using, let's use international drug trafficking. If we could have international wildlife trafficking be treated the same way to some extent as far as jurisdiction and enforcement, do you think that would help?

Mr. CRUDEN. Similar to what we have for drug trafficking.

Mr. POE. Similar to what we have for drug trafficking. Not kind of merge the laws. Make the laws very similar.

Mr. CRUDEN. I believe very clearly that wildlife trafficking, as you have stated, is a very serious crime similar to drug trafficking. And, therefore, we should be able to look at that and gain from that experience and benefit, and that might actually help us strengthen some of our laws. So I agree with you.

Mr. POE. And the same would be true of different terrorism laws because of the fact that these terrorist groups use the money to commit terror, maybe the Congress should explore expanding the trafficking issue because, as you have all said, this is a real problem. And it is the disappearance of certain wildlife soon if something is not done very quickly and effectively. Let me ask one more question, and I am going to yield to the ranking member for his questions.

45

What countries are the worst offenders as far as cooperating in preventing wildlife trafficking in their country? Nobody wants to say? I will ask you one specifically. How about Tanzania? Is Tanzania doing a good job of protecting the wildlife in their parks?

Mr. DREHER. I think the facts, there is an old saying about res ipsa loquitur. The issue here is that we know that recent data coming out of Tanzania from the Pan-African elephant survey shows that elephants are suffering enormous mortality in Tanzania and in their national parks in the areas of Selous and the Ruaha. They have a terrible poaching problem. And they are, at least at this point, from what we can tell, not able to control it. So they are working. We give them credit for engaging in this.

And we are working with them. I mean, our Ambassador in Tanzania is very much engaged in working with the government officials there, including providing assistance and training from AFRICOM. I mean, we are doing as many things as we can to try to strengthen their capacity, but they face an enormous challenge. Right now, I mean, as you may know, a year ago the Fish and Wildlife Service concluded it could not allow the import of sport hunting trophies of elephants from Tanzania because we could not conclude that their management of the populations in Tanzania was stable and sustaining. So all of those, I think, indicate that that is a country with serious challenges.

Mr. POE. And the biggest problem is in Central Africa and South Africa—is that a fair statement—of where the poaching is taking place?

Mr. Cruden, you nodded, so I will ask you.

Mr. CRUDEN. I want to nod, and remember I said in my opening statement that some of my comments are affected by what African leaders said. African leaders that I talked to talked about in Tanzania as a transshipment place, and your map that you gave us shows that. So not only do they have a problem, but it is a place where it goes to other places.

They also told us that they do go not directly to places like China or Vietnam because if you put China or Vietnam on your manifest, you are more likely to get checked at the customs office. So they put intermediary places like Malaysia or Philippines as a place that makes it less likely then that their illegal exportation of things like ivory will get looked at.

So I agree with everything that Mr. Dreher said, but I also think it is relevant as a transshipment place as well in this whole concept of organized crime.

Mr. POE. All right. Thank you. Mr. Keating.

Mr. KEATING. Thank you, Mr. Chairman.

The National Strategy for Combating Wildlife Trafficking specifically refers to the need for new technologies to identify poaching hot spots and trafficking patterns. It also calls on agencies to work with local communities to strengthen reporting of these activities. I am aware of some existing high-tech international partnerships between conservation organizations. For example, the International Fund for Animal Welfare and the Kenya Wildlife Service recently launched a project, tenBoma, to use geospatial monitoring and pattern analysis to predict and prevent poaching incidents before they happen. How does the State Department plan to integrate projects like these into its work?

Ambassador GARBER. Well, we certainly think that everybody has to be part of the solution, and new technologies and innovation is a key part of moving forward. And this is not the State Department per se, but this really is a whole-of-government approach; but my understanding, and I hope I am not going to do anything to steal someone's thunder, but it is my understanding that USAID today is going to be officially launching the Tech Challenge to be addressing this problem. So I hopefully won't have the Acting Administrator ready to take my head off by having announced that and maybe having stolen someone's thunder. I didn't see that it already happened today.

But we are working very closely with the NGO community trying to bring strong ways forward. We are doing this not just on wildlife trafficking, but you also talked about in your comments about illegal IUU fishing and ways to be approaching that. And we are going to be hosting a meeting in May with several of the NGOs to look at ways we can use some of these same new technologies to be addressing that question as well.

Mr. KEATING. Do other witnesses want to comment on some of the high-tech assistance we can get?

Mr. DREHER. There are varieties of tech, from high to low, that the folks in Africa that are fighting this problem really need. I mean, the high-tech things can include things as simple at night-vision scopes. A lot of the poachers are well-equipped, well-equipped with military surplus hardware. It can include relatively high-cost things like helicopters for aerial surveillance, but it can also include training and just making sure that the rangers are being paid decent living wages. So there is a whole range of things they need, but they clearly are outgunned and I think out-tech'd right now.

Mr. KEATING. Drone technology helpful at all?

Mr. CRUDEN. I mean, technology is—the GPS capability now, which is sweeping over Africa, will be enormously beneficial. They are working on fences. They are working on radar. They are using night-vision goggles, and all of those things are beneficial. But I will only, again, two things out of my Africa trip. One was a national park official telling me that their biggest challenge was they were outgunned. I thought maybe he was speaking metaphorically. I said, ''What do you mean?'' He said: ''I mean, they have rocket-propelled grenade launchers and automatic weapons, and we have World War II weapons.'' And so that was a challenge.

But also on not so high tech but just telling you what better coordination, we met with the local pilots association, you know, all over Africa. And we were in Botswana. There are hundreds of these small planes that are just couriering people back and forth. And the pilot I met with said:

> ''We are banding together. This is important to us. This is 15 percent of the gross national product of Botswana, and it pays for our salary. We are reporting to the government. We are getting together, and we will tell them when we see suspicious activity in the area because we know what strange vehicles look like, and we know what strange people look like.''

So I think the high tech really helps, but I also think that low-level activity can be enormously beneficial. And they are just getting there now.

Mr. KEATING. I know that the U.S. Fish and Wildlife, they have listed several potential changes in regulations related to ivory trade within the U.S., and many museums and antique dealers and scrimshanders are concerned that the rules could inadvertently but not drastically impact their trade while economically affecting U.S. consumers. When you are dealing with these regulations, will you be able to draw the lines clearly enough so there won't be any inadvertent effect?

Mr. DREHER. We are looking very closely at that. As you know, we are hoping to be able to get a draft rule out on the street very soon that would reflect the input we received from the interest groups that you have discussed and other folks that have, you know, well-intentioned interests that they are trying to maintain.

Our sole goal in trying to regulate the ivory trade in the United States is to eliminate the potential for it to serve as cover for illegal ivory. And there are di minimis amounts of ivory that are included, for example, in old musical instruments. And our goal is not to impede the movement of orchestras in and out of the United States. They are subject to CITES regulations, but we do everything we can to facilitate that. Similarly, we are going to do everything we can to accommodate truly di minimis uses of ivory. But the heart of the issue is, things that are multi-million-dollar antique ivory carvings are going to have to be able to demonstrate provenance. They are going to have to be able to demonstrate that they were not created, brought into the country, and then passed off as antique ivory. We had a major case just a year ago, where we—and John's folks successfully prosecuted an antiques dealer in Philadelphia who had a ton of ivory. And he was having it antiqued in Africa and shipped here to be passed off. That is what our concern is, is that our market here will end up being a front for illegal ivory. And we are going to do our best to cut down that kind of big-scale use.

Mr. KEATING. Lastly, in enforcement, it is so difficult because you are dealing with so many different nations. Some of them have varying degrees of rule of law. But one of the areas that you mentioned, Mr. Cruden, in terms of forfeiture, it is more administrative in nature. It is something that I think could be enforced a little better than a rule of law and actually going through judicial proceedings. Is there hope for that and getting into bank accounts and providing from enforcement people an incentive to go after these people in different countries?

Mr. CRUDEN. I want to answer in two ways: One of them is what we are doing; and, second, what we are promoting because, I told you, we are trying to do capacity building, and we are right now trying, working to set up programs in Africa. For us to be effective, for us to really deter illegal conduct, we have to make it not profitable. Even though we are seeking sentences, and we are putting people to jail. There is no question people are going to jail. That is not a bad deterrent effort, by the way, is putting you in jail. But that does not mean we are getting the higher network. That is what you do with RICO-like capability.

48

But when we are seeking restitution, when we are seeking to take the profit out of crime, right now what our statute does is we can actually do anything you do illegally. But some of these people are involved in a whole host of trafficking, some illegal, some not. And that would be one advantage is if we had a broader authority that we could take all of the profit out of it. But when we are going overseas—because sometimes it is very hard for them to come up with a penalty analysis, but it is not as hard for them to talk about restitution. It is not as hard to talk about seizing the assets of the illegal act. That is easier conceptually and easier for their courts to get their hands around. So not only is it valuable for us, but I think it is also valuable for us to explain and help and build capacity in some of these prosecutors that we are dealing with.

Mr. KEATING. And the timeframe can be drastically reduced, too.

Mr. CRUDEN. Yes, and the time frame is quickly reduced.

Mr. KEATING. I yield back.

Mr. POE. I have a couple of questions, and I am going to yield to a member that has joined us on the panel. I understand that, on Saturday, Thailand seized 4 metric tons of ivory. We have a Fish and Wildlife enforcement agent there in Bangkok. First of all, how many elephants would you have to kill to get 4 metric tons of ivory? All right. Somebody majored in math. Seriously, how many elephants are we talking about for 4 metric tons of ivory? Anybody have an idea, Mr. Dreher?

Mr. DREHER. My rule of thumb on this I think is that a tusk is about 20 pounds. So if you are talking about an adult elephant, 2 tusks, 40 pounds, to get to 4 metric tons, you are talking thousands of elephants that had to go into that shipment.

Mr. POE. So since we have an enforcement agent there in Bangkok from Fish and Wildlife, is there anything we can do to help Thailand track the criminal networks responsible for this slaughter of elephants?

Mr. DREHER. That is exactly why he is there. I wish I could take credit for the fact that it was our enforcement agent that helped bring this seizure to fruition, but I don't have that information. But what I can tell you is the reason we are placing attachés there and in the other locations we are proposing, all of which are hot spots for wildlife trafficking, is precisely to be able to coordinate with the law enforcement authorities of the country, with the other Federal agencies that are part of the Embassy and part of the mission there, and to try to coordinate this information.

Mr. POE. If I did my math right, there were 740 tusks at 20 bucks a piece. That is $14,800.

Ambassador GARBER. Our colleagues in the back who can actually do math better than me sitting here can actually do, are saying it is approximately 500 elephants.

Mr. POE. 500 elephants. Okay. I am going to ask unanimous consent that we have a Member that is not on the Foreign Affairs Committee ask questions, unless there is some objection, for Mr. DeFazio to be recognized for his question.

Mr. DEFAZIO. Thank you for not objecting, Mr. Chairman. I appreciate it.

First, I would observe, Mr. Chairman, that I did introduce a bill today we called—cleverly—called the TUSKER Act, H.R. 1945, that would require that countries that are identified under CITES as significant source, transit, or destination points for illegal ivory or rhino horn, immediately enter into consultations with the U.S. to discuss measures to end their importation and facilitation. Absent that, then the U.S. has the option of imposing sanctions. I think the Chinese with their, whatever their current trade deficit is with the U.S. at risk, would take some measures.

And I actually got some of the ideas from Jack Fields, former Republican Representative from Texas. You might know Jack. Jack worked on this on a bipartisan basis the last time we had a huge crisis. And we did pass a bill. It was particularly targeted at Hong Kong and some other areas at that point. They got the message pretty quickly, and it stopped. But, of course, now ivory is infinitely more valuable than it was then, and now you are talking about dealing with Lord's Resistance Army or ISIS or who knows who are financing their nefarious activities with this.

I would just put to the panel, I mean, first, I am not aware that, even though the President has CITES—has authority under Pelly, that he has thought about or has initiated any use of it against these target countries, even though we are initiating rules here. Secondly, if you are not aware of that, don't you believe that, given the fact that absent us sending in the SEALS and the Special Forces to level the playing field in terms of weaponry, that this is one of the best things the U.S. could do, which is to threaten meaningful sanctions against Vietnam, China, and the other major importers who are facilitating this trade.

So two questions, one, has there been any consideration or discussion of invoking Pelly, yes or no? And if not, would this not be potentially an effective tool?

Mr. DREHER. I am not aware of discussions within the administration of invoking Pelly. I know that it is an issue that from time to time is raised with us and that we do consider.

As to the issue of trade sanctions, I mean, a part of me wants to say that one of the great facts of coming to this hearing is that we are seeing people, including this committee—and we are very grateful for it—taking the wildlife trafficking crisis very seriously. And one of our messages has been throughout the National Strategy and our testimony here today that it should be considered to be on a par with other forms of extremely dangerous and lucrative international organized crime. And so we ask for the full strength of the government to be brought against it. I can't, however, give you any answer on the specific issue that you have raised for your bill about applying trade sanctions. There is a host of issues that would go into that, and I know that——

Mr. DEFAZIO. Sure. We always give into the Chinese, let them run a huge trade deficit, and steal our jobs. But maybe this is a time when we stand up for the last remaining elephants on Earth; send them a strong message; and say, ''Hey, you want us to pay you $200 billion more in deficit next year, well, guess what, not going to happen unless you''—and I know you can't go there with this administration, but since the administration has not shown any inclination to act meaningfully. It is one thing to go after some guy who was trying to bring a piano back into the U.S., and I did see that load of stuff, which was antiqued, and that was massive and huge, and I am glad you got him. But you need to be careful in writing this rule in terms of, you know, going so far that we end up—there is a provision Congress passed in the Gingrich era—rarely used—the Congressional Review Act, where every rule of major importance has to come to Congress for 60 days, and it can be essentially vetoed by Congress.

So the rule needs to be very thoughtfully done. I mean, when you get people excited about little, tiny embellishments in a gunstock and stuff like that, that is something we don't need. Thank you. Mr. Chairman.

Mr. DREHER. If I could just supplement my answer because I am informed that in fact we are looking at the issue of Pelly sanctions with regard to Vietnam and its role in the rhino horn trade, and we are also looking at Mozambique. So those things are being considered for those two countries.

Mr. DEFAZIO. Thanks. Let's look at China on ivory. I know it is tough to ever stand up to China, but we should do that.

Ambassador GARBER. If I could add and supplement what Mr. Dreher said, in our negotiations of the Trans-Pacific Partnership as well our negotiations with the European Union on possibly a transatlantic trade agreement, we are including environmental aspects, including wildlife trafficking, that would be subject and bound to dispute resolution and binding enforcement. So that is one tactic we are taking to look at the trade side.

And, specifically with regard to China, we have certainly been elevating the issue of wildlife trafficking in our engagement with the highest levels of Chinese Government. President Obama has raised it to President XI. I know that Secretary Kerry has raised it and will be using it again during a strategic and economic dialogue. I know that the Treasury Secretary raised it when he was just out in China last month. And I believe we have agreement to be raising it at the highest levels.

What we have found with China is that really significant change is going to have to come from the top down. We saw that with the success of shark fin. So we believe that we are really making some progress, and we are going to continue on a sustained basis raising this at the highest diplomatic levels.

Mr. DEFAZIO. I appreciate hearing that.

Thank you for your generous grant of time, Mr. Chairman.

Mr. POE. Thank you for being here.

One last comment following up on Ambassador Garber. China is by far the number one offending nation as far as where this ivory ends up. Is that a fair statement?

Ambassador.

Ambassador GARBER. Yes, that is our understanding.

Mr. POE. And then Vietnam would be the number one nation where rhino tusks end up. Is that correct?

Ambassador GARBER. Yes.

Mr. POE. Thank you all for being here. Members have 5 days to submit other questions and statements for the record.

And this subcommittee is adjourned. Thank you all.

[Whereupon, at 4 o'clock p.m., the subcommittee was adjourned.]

APPENDIX

MATERIAL SUBMITTED FOR THE RECORD

52

SUBCOMMITTEE HEARING NOTICE
COMMITTEE ON FOREIGN AFFAIRS
U.S. HOUSE OF REPRESENTATIVES
WASHINGTON, DC 20515-6128

Subcommittee on Terrorism, Nonproliferation, and Trade
Ted Poe (R-TX), Chairman

TO: MEMBERS OF THE COMMITTEE ON FOREIGN AFFAIRS

You are respectfully requested to attend an OPEN hearing of the Committee on Foreign Affairs, to be held by the Subcommittee on Terrorism, Nonproliferation, and Trade in Room 2172 of the Rayburn House Office Building (and available live on the Committee website at http://www.ForeignAffairs.house.gov):

DATE: Wednesday, April 22, 2015

TIME: 3:00 p.m.

SUBJECT: Poaching and Terrorism: A National Security Challenge

WITNESSES: The Honorable Judith G. Garber
Acting Assistant Secretary
Bureau of Oceans and International and Environmental and Scientific Affairs
U.S. Department of State

Mr. Robert Dreher
Associate Director
U.S. Fish and Wildlife Service
U.S. Department of the Interior

The Honorable John Cruden
Assistant Attorney General
Environment and Natural Resources Division
U.S. Department of Justice

By Direction of the Chairman

COMMITTEE ON FOREIGN AFFAIRS

MINUTES OF SUBCOMMITTEE ON _____*Terrorism Nonproliferation and Trade*_____ HEARING

Day_*Wednesday*_ Date_*April 22, 2015*_ Room_____*2172*_____

Starting Time _*3:00 p.m.*_ Ending Time _*4:00 p.m.*_

Recesses |___| (___to___) (___to___) (___to___) (___to___) (___to___) (___to___)

Presiding Member(s)

Chairman Ted Poe

Check all of the following that apply:

Open Session ☑   Electronically Recorded (taped) ☑
Executive (closed) Session ☐   Stenographic Record ☑
Televised ☑

TITLE OF HEARING:

"Poaching and Terrorism: A National Security Challenge"

SUBCOMMITTEE MEMBERS PRESENT:

Reps. Poe, Keating

NON-SUBCOMMITTEE MEMBERS PRESENT: *(Mark with an * if they are not members of full committee.)*

Rep. DeFazio*

HEARING WITNESSES: Same as meeting notice attached? Yes ☑ No ☐
(If "no", please list below and include title, agency, department, or organization.)

STATEMENTS FOR THE RECORD: *(List any statements submitted for the record.)*

Reps. Perry and Rohrabacher (Statements for the Record)

TIME SCHEDULED TO RECONVENE _____
or
TIME ADJOURNED _*4:00 p.m.*_

_____
Subcommittee Staff Director

Made in the USA
Las Vegas, NV
14 May 2022

48867193R00033